Re___'s Gift

TERECE HORTON

To my son Oliver,

Your strength and courage continue to amaze me and make me proud. Thank you for staying here with me. I love you more than words can express.

And for my grandson Jackson,

Thank you for your unconditional love and the joy you bring to my life. I love you always.

And thank you, God,

For all my blessings and the gift of Rebecca.

CONTENTS

ACKNOWLEDGMENTS

With deep gratitude and love to Mary Obana. Thank you for your book, *Shine*, and your guidance and enthusiastic encouragement to complete this book.

And with inexpressible thanks to my sister Tara Nickerson for being strong, capable, loving, and kind during my darkest days. Thank you for sharing your wisdom and writing expertise. I love you always.

INTRODUCTION

"Love is what we were born with. Fear is
what we learn. The spiritual journey is the
unlearning of fear and the acceptance of
love back in our hearts."

—MARIANNE WILLIAMSON

As a child, I had a wild and adventurous spirit. Despite this, messages of fear—*be careful, the world is not safe, you might get hurt,* and *life isn't fair*—gradually began to take over. Although coming from well-meaning sources—family, friends, and society—these messages were limiting and restrictive. Worry and anxicty accompanied them. Most of the time, I managed to push myself to do the things I wanted to do but often fear kept me from truly enjoying the experience. I remember when I was 28, standing on the top of Haleakala, a dormant volcano in Maui. The concern and worry about making the trip back down overshadowed the incredible beauty of the moment. It was as if I was always expecting something bad to happen. And then it did.

On May 28, 1994, my life was shattered. A drunk driver crashed into the car carrying my family. In one moment, my ex-husband Doug, his new wife Robin, and my eleven-year-old daughter, Rebecca, were killed. My nine-year-old son, Oliver, was trapped in the car with serious injuries.

I started writing this book in 1997 when my grief was still raw and deep. Searching for answers, I began interviewing rescue personnel, nurses, family, and friends. But as my life moved forward, I couldn't seem to find a way to finish. So one day, I put it in a box, where it has been for over twenty-two years. The pandemic of 2020 put my life on pause again. With time to spend alone and reflect, I was divinely guided to open the box I had avoided for so long and continue.

This is my story of grief and healing, and of how I found strength and courage, faith and trust, and ultimately the power of Love.

Rebecca's Gift

1
Innocence

MAY 24, 1994

"I got the front seat!" Rebecca and Oliver screamed at the same time, pushing and shoving each other as they both tried to sit in it.

"It's Oliver's turn today," I said firmly. With a little huff and a pout, Rebecca got in the back seat. "He always gets it," she declared, glaring at the back of his head.

"Just relax. We will be at the baseball game in five minutes," I replied, backing out of the driveway. Catching my eye as I smiled at her in the rear view mirror, she leaned forward as far as her seat belt would allow.

"Can I sing *Hero* for you?"

"Sure." I glanced at Oliver who rolled his eyes. For weeks, Rebecca had been practicing for the school concert and serenading us with Mariah Carey's song about inner strength. As we pulled into the ball field, she sang the last line about finding your way with time.

I smiled to myself. She was a born actress and loved to dance, living up to her sun sign Leo. Most Leos tend to be sunny, big-hearted, and comfortable being the center of attention. With a flair for the dramatic, she was always making up shows and directing her brother and their friends.

We got out of the car. Oliver was eager to play in his ball game and gave me a quick hug and kiss.

"Wait a minute, Oliver!" I grabbed his arm. "Did you forget? I'm leaving on vacation tonight. I'll see you in six days. Be good for Dad and Robin. I love you!"

As he ran off, Rebecca's shoulders slumped.

"I don't want you to go, Mom," she said, and she put her hand in mine as we walked toward the swings, away from the action of the ball game.

Rebecca was wearing my gray work sweatshirt with her jean shorts and her long blond hair hung straight down her back. I stroked it, feeling the softness. She was growing into a lovely young lady, tall like me and seeming older than her years. She had a zest for life and lived every moment to the fullest.

"I don't want you to miss me singing in chorus on Thursday," she pleaded. It would be the first time I would miss one of her performances. I loved seeing Rebecca perform. Although I would be back in time to see her star in the sixth-grade play and then dance in her year-end recital, I still felt guilty. It was hard to say good-bye. I had never left my children for more than a weekend. But at 40, I felt that I needed some time for myself. For the first time since my divorce and my graduation from Bancroft School of Massage Therapy, life seemed open to new possibilities. When my friend Suzanne told me she was going to Colorado to visit her son and invited me, I accepted. I was always drawn to the beauty of the Southwest with its majestic, mysterious mountains and sacred, healing, spiritual places. It seemed to be calling me now.

"I'll break a bone!" Rebecca said. "That will get you back here!"

I couldn't help cringing a little as my own fears set in. Rebecca knew me so well. I was a worrier.

"Rebecca, you don't have to break a bone. If you need me, I'll come home. I love you so much."

She started to cry. I hugged her and was glad for this time alone. It was unlike her to be so upset. She loved spending time with her dad and was accustomed to our arrangement. When we divorced in 1991, Doug and I had agreed on joint custody. He moved close by so we could both be involved with our children on a daily basis. They stayed with me four nights and spent three at his new house.

"Here comes Robin!" I said, as I saw her coming across the field toward us. Doug's new wife had short brown hair and a pleasant face that made me warm up to her instantly. Although they had only been married for six months, Robin was kind and loving with my children and was a welcome addition to our family. Rebecca wiped her eyes, smiled and looked up.

"Rebecca is having a hard time. Thanks for taking care of her," I told Robin and gave her a hug. Then I hugged and kissed Rebecca.

"'Bye, honey. I love you. I'll miss you."

"'Bye, Mommy. I love you too."

Driving away from the ballfield, I sensed an uneasy feeling creep into my body. I was always nervous and worried when I was away from my kids. But this heavy feeling came from a place deep within. I turned on the radio and tried to ignore it, rationalizing that my fears were getting the best of me.

Suzanne and I spent two days in Boulder. The magnificent mountains reflected both strength and peace to me. I soaked up the vibrant colors of yellow, turquoise, blues, reds, and the many shades of brown and tried to relax and experience the Southwestern culture that I've always loved. We shopped, talked, walked, and ate at a local Mexican restaurant. I am drawn to Indian art and silver jewelry with the little Kokopellis. But my heart wouldn't allow me to fully enjoy myself. I bought Rebecca a turquoise T-shirt and purple velvet ribbon for her hair. I couldn't find a gift for Oliver. The strong urge to be home seemed to pervade everything. I missed the kids and wanted to be with them.

On Friday, May 26, we drove to Fort Collins, where Suzanne and her son dropped me off at the home of Christy, a friend from my waitressing days on Cape Cod. After a visit with her husband, Mike, and their two daughters, Christy and I went to Poudre Canyon to take a walk along the river. The steep walls and layers of reddish rock were such a contrast to the flatness of scrub pines and sandy beaches of Cape Cod. I felt the beauty deep inside. I could almost hear the chanting of ancient voices. The sun filtered through the trees as we hiked, both of us lost in thought. Christy climbed up on a boulder, and I joined her, basking in the late afternoon sun. As the water rushed by, we talked about our children—our fears and concerns for them. We both agreed that, although difficult at times, motherhood was the most fulfilling part of our lives. For some reason I mentioned a friend whose little girl was run over by a school bus in front of her house a few years ago. That tragedy had affected me deeply. Christy and I couldn't imagine how anyone could go on after losing a child. In tune with our mood, the air turned chilly as the sun started to go down. We headed back to Christy's house.

Early that evening, the phone rang and Christy picked it up. I heard her say "Is this Rebecca?" and then, "Yes, your mom is here." She smiled and handed me the phone.

"Hi, Mom." It was so good to hear her voice.

"Hi, honey," I said. "How was your concert?"

"It was good. I wished you were there." I could hear the regret in her voice.

"I'm sorry." I replied. I hated missing it too.

"Please come home now," she pleaded. She sounded so sad.

"I'll be home soon. I miss you and I love you so much," I told her. My heart hurt.

"I love you too, Mom. Here's Daddy."

Doug got on the phone. He said all was well, but he was tired. He was taking the kids to New Hampshire tomorrow to his friend Phil's fortieth birthday party. It would be a quick trip up and back because Sunday was Doug's annual Memorial Day Cookout. What a long trip for a short visit,

I thought. It's a three-and-a-half-hour drive one-way to Wolfboro. But I knew better than to offer Doug my opinion. I also knew Doug had a creed. He didn't leave the Cape on Memorial Day weekend. "Why fight traffic when you have the best of everything right here?" he would say. It bothered me that Doug would make an exception now. But what could I do?

Friday night, Christy and her family took me to Fort Collins to show me the town. While stopped at a red light, we were suddenly rear-ended by a young cowboy in his father's pickup truck. The unexpected impact and the loud sound of crunching metal was frightening. Although no one was seriously hurt, Christy would later suffer from severe whiplash. We were all trembling and quite shaken up. On the quiet drive home, we commented on how life can change in an instant.

On Saturday, May 28, Christy invited a friend and her children for a picnic at a nearby pond. With all the kids around, I missed Rebecca and Oliver even more. I rowed out to the middle of the pond alone and again was overcome with anxiety and worry for no discernable reason. Later, Christy and her friend had a brief conversation about a teacher and mother in town who had been killed by a drunk driver. We all agreed how terrible, sad, and senseless that was.

That afternoon, I went upstairs to the loft over the kitchen to take a nap. Six-year-old April came up for a visit. We lazed on the bed and talked about angels. She reminded me of Rebecca with her questions and inquisitiveness. Later, when Christy had her sing *Somewhere over the Rainbow*, her sweetness and willingness to perform made me think of Rebecca again.

That evening, Christy and I went out for Mexican food and margaritas. We came home early and I went to bed, setting the alarm for 6:00 a.m. for a hike in Estes Park.

The ringing of a phone woke me. It was still dark. I looked at the clock on the nightstand next to the ringing phone. It was 4:30 a.m. It was not my house, so I didn't answer it. I was sure someone would pick it up. I didn't want to. It continued to ring and ring. The persistent shrill finally made me pick it up.

"Hello?"

I heard my sister's voice say, "I need to talk to Terece."

I said, "Tara, this is me."

She told me softly and hesitantly.

"There has been a bad accident. Doug, Robin, and . . . Rebecca have been killed. Oliver is badly injured, and you need to come home. He needs you."

*   *   *

APRIL 2020

Looking back, years later, I see events and conversations in that trip that may have been signals or signs. There were too many to be coincidences. They seemed to be gentle reminders of a plan, God's plan. A Divine Blueprint, not only preparing, but protecting me. I believe that on some level, Rebecca knew she was leaving. Even if she wasn't consciously aware of it, her soul was. To this day, twenty-six years later, the song she sang to me of finding inner strength haunts and heals me.

"God's Heavenly Plan doesn't always make Earthly sense."

—CHARLES SWINDOLL

2
Devastation

Deep in my being, I knew this was what I had been afraid of. I whispered "Tara, how can this be true?"

"The police are here at my house. They don't know Oliver's condition," she explained. "He has been airlifted to a hospital in Boston."

"Please go and be with him," I said. "I'm coming home."

I hung up the phone.

The room was dark and silent. Maybe I was dreaming. No, my heart was beating too hard. I got out of bed and stumbled down the stairs, grasping the railing to find my way in the darkness. At the bottom, I felt along the walls for a light switch. It was hard to breathe. I couldn't find the light. I groped my way feeling the furniture like a blind woman in unknown territory. By the time I got to Christy and Mike's bedroom, I was crawling. Shaking, I climbed onto the end of their bed.

"What?" they both cried at once and stared at me in the dim light.

"There has been an accident." I immediately saw the horror in their faces and added, "Heather and April are fine. . . It's Rebecca. . . she's been killed. I need to go home right away. Help me."

They both looked at me in disbelief and confusion.

"Didn't you hear the phone ring?" I asked.

"No. There isn't a phone at this end of the house," Christy said, her voice getting high-pitched and shaky.

I repeated what Tara had just told me on the phone. Christy went to check on her girls. Reassured that they were safe, she came back and told me, "I'll call Suzanne and Mike will call the airport. Go get dressed."

I moved in slow motion. *This can't be happening*, I thought. While putting on a shirt and jeans, my colon began to spasm. I rushed to the bathroom.

When I was finally dressed, I opened my suitcase. Christy came in and began throwing in my clothes.

"No! I need to do this." I slowly folded a pair of jeans and carefully placed them in the suitcase. It seemed very important to do this neatly and orderly. When I finished, it was hard to breathe again.

"I'm going outside to get some air. Could you call my mother and tell her I'm okay?"

I stepped out alone into the Colorado morning. The glow from the sun coming up over the trees filled the gray-blue sky with yellow and pink stripes, like streamers at a little girl's birthday party. Birds were chirping. Everything seemed so alive with anticipation of the new day. Why was the world going on without me? I walked down the deserted street and tried to catch my breath. Looking up at the sky, I knew I had to make the choice to go on. I just couldn't imagine how.

Christy caught up with me a few houses down from hers. She started to cry and said, "Suzanne is on her way here and will take you home. I'm riding to the airport with you and I'll take the bus back. I talked to your mom. She and your father will pick you up in Boston and take you to the hospital."

Time seemed to slow down as we walked up and down that street, waiting for Suzanne and the long trip home.

When Suzanne arrived, she took me in her arms. Her warmth and concern momentarily soothed me.

"Where is Doug?" she wanted to know. I told her he and Robin had been killed too.

"Oh my God, you mean a car accident?" She gasped, shock and horror reflected in her big brown eyes. Again she pulled me to her. Her strength helped to keep me standing.

It is a ninety-minute drive to the Denver International Airport from Fort Collins. Suzanne drove the little red rental car. I stared vacantly out the window as worries about Oliver and his injuries tormented me. We didn't have much information. The Rocky Mountains we had hoped to climb seemed distant and gray-looking. Clouds drooped over them as if they were reflecting my sadness.

When we arrived at the rental car return, Christy ran into the bathroom and got sick. We both needed fresh air and sat outside at the curb. Suzanne finished the paperwork and then we all got on the shuttle bus together. On the way to the terminal, I started to cry.

"Rebecca can't be dead," I repeated over and over again.

A pretty, dark-haired woman holding a beautiful red rose sat across from me. I focused on the rose, mesmerized. I could tell it was special to her by the way she was holding it, carefully and lovingly.

At the airport ticket counter, Suzanne turned to me and said we had to make a decision. We could leave in a half-hour on a flight that had two seats available with a changeover in Cincinnati or go on standby for a non-stop flight an hour later. Never a big risk taker and feeling the urgency to get on a plane, I was very clear. "Take the sure thing."

As I waited for Suzanne to get our tickets, the woman from the shuttle bus approached me slowly. She handed me the red rose and said, "I think you need this more than me." I burst into tears and told her my daughter had been killed.

"I'm sorry," she murmured softly, as her own eyes filled with tears.

I clutched that rose for the whole five-hour flight.

Now that I knew our flight, I called my parents to tell them we would be arriving at 5:00 p.m. I asked my mother if she knew more about Oliver. She told me he had a broken leg and lung and head injuries, and that he had been airlifted to New England Medical Center. I knew then that his condition was life-threatening.

Christy kept saying, "Oliver will be okay," over and over until we got to security. She hugged me goodbye, and

Suzanne and I continued on toward our boarding gate. I passed a gift shop and remembered I didn't have a gift for Oliver. Maybe he would be okay if I bought something. I ran in frantically and found him a blue T-shirt with an eagle and a cougar on it, animals that symbolize strength.

Finally we boarded the plane. Throughout the flight I prayed and chanted an affirmation, "I believe in the miracle of healing," over and over again.

Suzanne's presence was a great comfort. Suzanne and I had met four years ago at Massage Therapy School and had quickly become close friends. We both shared a quest for healing and spirituality. After graduation she moved to Cape Cod and opened a massage practice in Osterville. A few months later, I joined her business. Suzanne was a beautiful woman with big brown eyes and a vibrant personality. She was eight years my senior, and I always thought of her as a wise woman and valued her ideas and friendship.

She tried to reassure me: "Oliver will be okay. He has to be."

When we finally arrived in Cincinnati, I was really feeling sick. In the airport, I tried to get some soup to settle my stomach, but we couldn't find any. I didn't want to eat anything else. My legs felt weak; I thought I would pass out. I felt I needed air, but there was no door to get outside at the concourse. Suzanne kept pushing me on until it was time to board our flight to Boston.

As we were getting on the plane, I couldn't catch my breath. I saw a small opening between the jetway ramp and the plane. I crouched down and breathed in a small stream of air. It felt as if I were suffocating. The urge to be outside was overwhelming. Suzanne had to explain to the stewardess what was wrong with me, and she gently guided us to our seats.

Once we were settled, I prayed that Oliver would not be on a respirator and would not have brain damage. I continued to hold my rose and quietly chant, "I believe in the miracle of healing," until we landed in Boston. Suzanne helped me off the plane.

My family was standing there when we came down the ramp. My mother came up and put her arms around me.

"How could this happen?" I cried into her shoulder. My brothers, John and Jason, and my father stood quietly by us. Although they were silent, I could feel their love and support.

Dad drove to New England Medical Center. When we got there, John ushered us in the back way, saying something about avoiding the police and news media.

"What?" I asked. "Police, news reporters, why?"

"The man who smashed Doug's car had been traveling the wrong way down the highway at high speed and was presumed to be under the influence. He fled the scene of the accident, and there is a manhunt going on," he explained.

We arrived outside the intensive care unit. Tara and my friend Jane were there. They introduced me to Sister Claire from the pastoral care department. I was afraid to see Oliver. Could I handle it? If the kids needed stiches or a shot, Doug was the one who dealt with it. I wondered how I was going to tell Oliver about Rebecca, Daddy, and Robin.

"Does he look bad?" I asked Tara.

"No, but he's not conscious," she replied.

Jane told me that they had just taken him off the respirator.

Whispering "Thank you, God," I took a deep breath and prepared myself to enter the pediatric intensive care unit, a place no parent should ever have to visit.

$$\star \quad \star \quad \star$$

MAY 2020

I continue to see the Divine plan being revealed and how that includes Divine timing. The distance of Colorado had given me some solace. Time had stopped for me. I truly had to live in the present moment, step by step, one breath at a time. That was all I could handle. I needed to take in the shock and gather my inner strength and faith to be there for Oliver and to be able to cope with his pain and suffering as well as my own. And keep making that choice to go on.

I see how my family, friends, and even strangers were angels placed, like lights in the darkness, on my path. Their kindness, comfort, guidance, and love carried me through those first dark days and continue to heal me.

One of those angels was Jim Kelley. He came to my house in April of 1997 and told me his story.

> **"We are each of us angels with only one wing.**
> **And we can only fly embracing each other."**
> —LUCIANO DE CRESCENZO

3
Angels

That Saturday night of Memorial Day weekend, Jim Kelley, a 911 Boston police officer, was on his way home to the Cape. Although it had rarely happened before, Jim's relief had shown up late for the next shift, delaying him an extra 15 minutes. It was about 11:30 p.m., and he was almost through Plymouth when he saw brake lights and a cloud of smoke that looked like a bomb had gone off. Then he realized there had been a horrific accident. There were at least three cars involved, one of them nearly crushed at the guard rail. The crash must have happened only moments before, Jim thought, as there were no rescue personnel on the scene yet. Then a Plymouth police officer arrived. Jim knew what they had to do.

The first vehicle's occupants were an elderly couple, both conscious. The second car, a Chevy Blazer, was headed in the direction opposite the flow of traffic and was empty. They hurried to the third vehicle. The impact of the crash had almost buried the occupants in twisted metal. Jim thought they all must be dead. The back section of the car's roof had been pried off like the lid of a sardine can. Then he saw the two children in the back seat, a girl and a boy. Miraculously they were still alive, but drifting in and out of consciousness. They were both trapped in the contorted wreckage that the two police officers were powerless to budge, much less pry away.

The little boy opened his eyes and began to wail, an unearthly, high-pitched keening filled with pain and terror. As unsettling as the sound was, and as much as he hoped the youngster didn't realize what was going on, Jim felt relieved. If the boy could cry like that, he was obviously getting enough oxygen into his lungs.

The little girl was another story. She was situated on the passenger side, the side that had sustained the most damage. She appeared to be having trouble breathing, and her lips were already beginning to turn a tell-tale blue. Her eyelids fluttered open, then closed. Her long, pale blond hair was the same color as Jim's little girl's.

Jim's instincts took over, not as a police officer, but as a father. He crawled next to her. "I'm here," he said. "It's all right." He stroked her face, the only part he could reach. He had never felt so powerless in his life. Beside him, the little boy continued to scream. "Hang on, little guy," Jim told him. "We'll get you out of here." He didn't see how either one of the children could possibly make it.

The little girl's eyes fluttered open once more, then shut. Her struggle to breathe became more labored, her lips bluer. A few minutes later, she died.

Firefighters arrived and began to cut through the wreckage. At least an hour or so later, the little boy with the silky brown hair and long eyelashes, the sole survivor of a crash that had destroyed his family, was in an ambulance on his way to the hospital. No one at the scene held out much hope for his survival.

Another police officer, Jeff Chase, was working that night at the Barnstable Police Station on Cape Cod. He had switched shifts as a favor so a co-worker could have the night off. He went in at 4:00 a.m. His first call was to meet a state trooper at Burger King to go and help him make a notification of a bad accident in Plymouth with multiple fatalities. He needed to find Terece Horton, who lived in Marstons Mills. When Jeff heard the name he said, "I know Terece, and I know where she lives." The trooper explained that the driver, Douglas Horton, a woman, and a young girl had been killed. A little boy was in real tough shape and they needed to find Terece as soon as possible. They rushed to my house. Although my car was in the yard, no one came to the door.

Jeff wasn't aware at the time that Doug and I were divorced and he was remarried. Discovering I wasn't home, Jeff went to my neighbor and friend Jane's house. Jane's daughter and Jeff's daughter were friends.

After Jeff told Jane what had happened, she got hysterical. But eventually she was able to explain that I was in Colorado. She knew my sister Tara would have a phone number to contact me, as this was before everyone had cell phones.

They arrived at Tara's house at 6:00 in the morning.

*   *   *

MAY 2020

As difficult and almost unbearable as it was for me to hear Jim and Jeff's story, I felt some peace and gratitude knowing Rebecca and Oliver were not alone. It was as if God had placed Jim with my children when I couldn't be there to comfort them. For Jim to be the first on the scene and for Jeff to have to do the notification must have had a big emotional impact on them. I can't imagine. Again, the coincidences, synchronicities, and timing show how connected we all are. So many lives were entwined to help and be there for one another. I know the trauma Jim, Jeff, and all the rescue personnel had to experience will be with them always. Thank you all for caring, helping, being with Rebecca, and saving Oliver.

"Remember, I am always with you."

—MATTHEW 28:20

4
Messages

MAY 29, 1994

Sister Claire, from the Pastoral Care Department, was a woman not much older than I. She glowed with a love and warmth that drew me into her arms. Then, taking my hand, she guided me through the heavy, white, foreboding doors.

The eerie silence and medicinal smells of the intensive care unit permeated my senses. It was a large, dark room with rows of beds and cribs, some with curtains drawn around them as if to hide the worst. Two nurses stood near a station with charts, phones, and strange-looking equipment. I could feel their sympathetic eyes watching me as Sister Claire led me to a bed across the room. A small boy with brown hair lay at an awkward angle on the white sheets. His head was tilted back and one leg was held up by a triangular-shaped device.

Could this be my active, happy Oliver? Was this all that was left of my family? A voice screamed inside my head. I couldn't move, afraid to touch him. A nurse came over and softly spoke.

"It's okay. Hold his hand and let him know you are here."

Slowly reaching down, I took his limp little hand in mine. There was a red light attached to his thumb. Tubes came out of his nose. Trembling, I took a breath. In a shaky voice I said, "Mommy's here." I stroked his hand.

Suddenly, Oliver opened his eyes and looked around wildly. He screamed, "They're all dead! They're all dead! Put the car back together! Put the car back together!"

He knew. My heart stopped. I could only imagine the horror he had experienced.

"I know, I know," I told him. "I love you. Mommy's here. I'll take care of you."

He fell back and drifted off again. I kept talking softly, telling him I would take care of him, wondering how I would. I clung to his hand. I didn't want to ever let it go. For a while, he drifted in and out of consciousness.

At one point he yelled, "Take the bracelet off." He clawed at the tube going across his face into his nose.

I was frightened for him. I was frightened for me.

The night passed in a blur. Suzanne and Tara stayed and took shifts at Oliver's bedside with me. Oliver slept most of the time. When he did wake up, he would look around anxiously and then get calm when he saw me. I didn't want to leave his side.

In the predawn hours, I watched the silent ministering of the nurses. It all seemed so unreal, like the set of a horror movie. I noticed a baby with a large bandage around her head in a crib. She lay there staring at nothing. I felt so sad for her. On the other side of the room was a young girl about Rebecca's age. She was very still. I couldn't look at her for long because I was afraid to think about Rebecca. Where was Rebecca? I was glad she was with Doug. I knew he would take care of her. I knew they were safe with God in heaven. But I didn't really understand.

Sister Claire wanted me to rest. She took me to a small room, a cubicle with no windows and a wooden bench. I lay there on the hard bench in the empty room feeling like a prisoner being punished for a crime I didn't commit. Stabbing pains in my stomach kept me awake. Shaking, alone in the dark, I wondered, *Will I ever be able to sleep again?*

In the morning, I was still unable to eat or sleep. Sister Claire arranged for me to get a sedative. Then, only after I was assured my two brothers would stay with Oliver and not leave his side, I left with Suzanne for the Cape. I was needed to make funeral arrangements.

Suzanne drove. During the ninety-minute drive, I dozed off just before we passed the scene of the accident on Route 3 at Exit 3, six miles from the Sagamore Bridge. At my parent's house, I went in and fell asleep in the guest room. As I was drifting off, I thought about my house. It was only ten minutes away. How could I go back there without Rebecca? It was our home. We all lived there together.

I woke up a few hours later. I wanted to get back to Oliver. He was all I could think about. Like a zombie, I showered and went down to the kitchen. My mother snatched some newspapers off the table.

"Don't look at those!" my mother exclaimed, as she quickly hid them. She gave me eggs and toast, and I was finally able to eat. I called the hospital to get a report on Oliver and talk to my brothers.

"Good news," John told me. "Oliver is going to be moved to a regular room."

"Tell him I'll be there as soon as I can." I slowly let out my breath, feeling a little lighter. He wasn't critical anymore. He would be all right.

My parents drove me to the funeral home. We met the young priest filling in for our parish head that weekend. His quiet presence helped to calm the disbelief and confusion. Doug's mom, Margo, and Robin's parents were there. Margo and I hugged each other for a long time. We had always been close and understood each other. Now we had a stronger bond. We had both lost a child.

Decisions had to be made quickly, starting with choosing the coffins. I couldn't. I wasn't ready to face that. My mother focused on the music. She suggested *On Eagle's Wings*, knowing I liked eagles because of their strength.

"That's fine," I said. "But we have to sing *Hero* for Rebecca. She's been singing it to me for months." Maybe that was a premonition, I thought.

I felt bad for Robin's mom. A kind-looking woman with short brown hair like Robin's, she stared vacantly, her husband at her side. She hardly knew us, and here we all were planning a triple wake and funeral together. To say this was overwhelming doesn't come close to describing the state we were in. I couldn't focus. My eyes drifted from one pain-filled face to another. No one wanted to look at brochures on coffins. Everyone was being nice to each other when we really just didn't want to be there.

I was finally ready to leave the funeral home. My friend Mary had come to pick me up and take me back to the hospital in Boston. The ride in her red Ford Bronco felt familiar. It was something I had done many times over the past ten years we had worked together. The comfort and familiarity was quickly replaced by the shocking thought that nothing would ever be the same again. I loved my job, counseling pregnant women and mothers at the Women, Infants, and Children Nutrition Education Program (WIC). I wondered if I would ever work again. Everything seemed to be in a haze. The little energy I had, even for thoughts, was focused on Oliver and getting back to him.

It felt safe to be back in the confines of the hospital. Oliver's new room was already filled with cards. Colorful balloons hung from the ceiling. I thanked my brothers, who after reporting that he had been sleeping most of the time, went to take a break. As I sat next to him, stroking his tangled and matted hair, I found a couple slivers of glass and then I discovered a tick.

"Oh, Mary, quick, help me get this tick off him!"

She quickly found and removed three of them. We figured they must have got on him in New Hampshire the day of the accident. It struck me then that tick bites were not a worry compared to his life-threatening injuries, and the enormity of the situation hit me again. It was a miracle that he had survived. What would I have done if he hadn't? He was all that was keeping me going.

One of the nurses from Oliver's team at New England Medical Center came to explain his condition to me.

"Oliver's head injury had been the immediate concern and had been carefully attended to by the rescue personnel to prevent brain swelling. It seems okay now, but we'll have to wait to see if there is brain damage."

My breathing slowed as I said a silent prayer.

She continued on, "After his prolonged extraction from the car, he was first brought to Jordan Hospital in Plymouth, stabilized, and then flown by a helicopter med-flight to Boston. They did not know his name so he was listed as John Doe. Later, when he was asked his name, it sounded like he said Christopher. So he was Christopher Doe for his first few hours at New England Medical Center. They took X-rays, CAT scans and tests. He was operated on immediately for a hip fracture, and two pins were inserted in the neck of his femur. He also has a pulmonary contusion which is being monitored. He is now stabilized and is expected to make a full recovery, physically."

Physically? I thought, after she left the room. How would he handle this emotionally? Oliver had a speech delay and had been hard to understand until he was six. His lack of communication skills and sensitive personality kept me often catering to his needs. In contrast, Rebecca seemed to be independent almost from birth. I thought of all the times I had said to her, "Wait, Rebecca. Oliver needs me." Now I was asking her to wait again. His needs were immediate, so grieving for her would have to come later. I couldn't handle both.

Oliver's healing continued. He smiled at me when he was awake and he moved around more on the bed. I was so glad he was out of intensive care. I had never let in the thought that he had almost died, too. I knew he would live. He had to. We needed each other. From the beginning, his will to live gave me strength. The fact that he could smile at me after all he had been through gave me such hope. I could do this.

I never let Oliver or myself be alone during his hospital stay. We both needed the support, and I was afraid to be in charge. There was always a loving friend or family member with us. Jason had stayed on with Mary and me, so he was with Oliver when the two of us went down to the cafeteria in the morning.

The hospital cafeteria is on the ground floor and has doors that open up to a courtyard and walkway in the busy city of Boston. After breakfast, I craved fresh air again. We went outside. The sun was so bright it was almost blinding. Honking horns, loud engines, and voices filled the air. I noticed the many homeless people wandering around the area. I thought about my own home and how far away it seemed. I turned to go back inside. Almost magically, a glint of light caught my eye. I looked down at my feet. There were two shiny dimes side by side.

"Look, Mary!" I said and reached down to pick them up. She knew my habit of picking up pennies to read the dates and was not surprised. But we were both shocked and amazed at the dates on the dimes. The first one was 1982, the year Rebecca was born. The second one was 1994, which is now the year of her death. I immediately felt it was a sign to let me know she was okay. I felt like she was watching me.

"Thank you," I whispered, and then hugged Mary.

We both knew it was more than an unusual coincidence, it was a miracle.

★   ★   ★

May 2020

The definition of a miracle is "an effect or extraordinary event in the physical world that surpasses all known human or natural powers and is ascribed to a supernatural cause," "a work of God," a "wonderful thing."

There were so many miracles, all of them wonderful. The most important was Oliver's survival and accelerated healing; Tara and Jane both remarked on his many bruises and how by the time I arrived they were beginning to fade. One of the first miracles, clear to me, was the woman with the red rose; a red rose symbolizes an expression of love, and it can be used to convey heartfelt regret and sorrow. The coins with Rebecca's birth and death dates will always amaze me; with all the people around, no one else had picked them up. These signs all gave me hope and encouragement. And little did I realize an even bigger miracle was yet to come.

> "There are only two ways to live your life.
> One is as though nothing is a miracle.
> The other is as though everything
> is a miracle."
>
> —ALBERT EINSTEIN

5
Remembrance

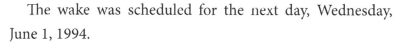

MAY 31, 1994

The wake was scheduled for the next day, Wednesday, June 1, 1994.

"I need to look good for Rebecca," I said, turning to Mary for answers.

"I know," she replied. "I am going to take you to buy a new dress." Jason agreed to stay with Oliver.

Leaving the safety of the hospital felt strange to me, like being in unknown territory. We walked down Boston's busy Kneeland Avenue in the heart of Chinatown. Crowds of people rushed along, bumper-to-bumper cars sat with their motors idling, horns blared, and sirens screamed. The noise and confusion made me want to cover my ears. I stared at some women walking by us. It astonished me that they were going about their business while my life had come to a standstill. I wanted to shout at them, "Don't you know what has happened to my family?!"

Mary and I had shopped many times before, but Filene's seemed like a foreign land. I could not believe we were looking for a dress for Rebecca's wake and funeral. Mary, familiar with my taste, immediately picked out three dresses. The first one was perfect. I am tall, and the delicate rayon draped my body in a way that made me feel regal. The dress was an Indian print, and I loved the colors. The background was teal green with purple, pink, and gold designs. There were little beads around the neck, and a vest of the same print. Mary wanted to buy it for me. She quickly picked out pink beaded earrings to match.

Early that evening, Sister Claire came to Oliver's room and asked me to come to the lounge with her.

"I'd like to talk to you about the wake," she said, and then gently asked, "Have you thought about seeing Rebecca's body?"

"Her body? No! How could I? I don't think I want to," I cried in a shocked voice. "It would be too hard, too painful. What if she looks terrible? I don't want that to be my last memory." My eyes filled with tears.

Sister Claire agreed it would be difficult. I didn't even want to consider it.

"No!" I said emphatically. She softly encouraged me to give it some thought.

Later that night, Sister Claire came back again. She explained,

"It is important that you see Rebecca. It will be your last chance. It will, in time, help you to accept Rebecca's death."

Early the next morning, the day of Rebecca, Doug, and Robin's wake, the parents of Oliver's best friend, Nathaniel, came to stay with Oliver. I thanked them and told them they would be relieved by Stacy and her boyfriend around suppertime. Stacy had been Rebecca and Oliver's babysitter since they were infants, and she was like a member of our family. She even looked like Rebecca and me with her straight honey-blond hair and glasses. My children loved Stacy. She had agreed to stay with Oliver until the next day when I returned after the funeral. I knew Oliver would be content with Stacy. I left for the Cape.

The wake was from 2:00 to 4:00 p.m. and 7:00 to 9:00 p.m. My parents and I arrived around 1:30 p.m. Huge bouquets of colorful flowers filled the room with their beauty and sweet aroma. I was amazed and drawn to all the roses. There was one cluster of deep-red roses that really stood out. I focused on them. Then, moving like a robot going through the motions, I hugged and greeted members of all three families that were there before the public arrived. Someone told me I had to see Rebecca and Doug now before the doors opened and the coffins would be closed. Robin's body had taken the brunt of the crash and could not be viewed by anyone but her immediate family.

I walked into the room. The three coffins loomed ominously ahead. Rebecca lay in the first one. She had on the cream-colored dress with little pink roses that I had bought her to wear in her chorus performance, the one that I had missed. Her beautiful, long blond hair was shining like a light around her. I felt my life flowing from my body. I fell to my knees, crying.

"My baby, my baby!"

But a force drew me to her. I slowly rose and reached for her. I touched her hair. It was soft and clean as if it had been freshly washed and brushed. She looked so young and still. I continued to stroke her hair. Her face and body seemed fine. Why wasn't she jumping up to kiss me, putting her arms around me, telling me she loved me? Where was she?

Time was running out. The funeral director wanted to open the doors. Margo came over and brought me to Doug's side. He looked good, even with the bruises on his face. I touched him. I kissed Doug good-bye and then went back and kissed Rebecca. I wanted to hold her in my arms once more, but there wasn't time. Someone led me away. I never saw her again.

The coffins were closed, and a photograph was placed on each one. The picture of Rebecca had been taken when she was ten, before her braces. She had on a white, wide-rimmed Easter bonnet and a pink and blue Nordic-looking sweater. Her head was tilted to one side, her blue eyes dancing and her sweet smile reaching right into your heart. Doug's photo was from the day of his wedding to Robin, six months previously. He was in his tuxedo with Oliver sitting on his lap. Doug's eyes were gleaming and his head thrown back in laughter. The picture of Robin was from their wedding day, too. She was glowing, radiant, and smiling.

The doors to the John-Lawrence Funeral Home opened. For two hours, I hugged, cried, kissed, and greeted hundreds of adults and children. It was all surreal. I felt as if *I* were consoling *them*, especially the children. Rebecca's friends and classmates looked as lost and frightened as I was. Hugging and comforting them seemed to console me, too. Most faces were familiar, but others I didn't know. Everyone looked sad and shocked; many were crying. And then it was over.

We went back to my parent's house. I heard someone say, "I need a drink." I felt a rush of anger. Drinking was what killed my family. Didn't they get it? I could not make small talk. I went to lie down and fell asleep.

Back at the wake at 6:30, I was in even more of a stupor. I stood, hugged, and consoled, again. Toward the end of the two hours, the funeral director brought the three mothers, Margo, Nancy, and me to a private room. We had to discuss cemetery plot plans and the burial. This was almost too much for me. Not now. Feeling totally confused, I wanted to run from the room, but then a thought came in clear and strong. I looked at Margo and said, "I think Doug would have wanted to be cremated."

I wasn't sure where those words came from, but I felt I had been guided. I knew it was the truth. Margo agreed, and I decided Rebecca would be cremated, too.

Going back to my parent's house, slumped in the backseat, I wondered about cremation. I had never really given it much thought before. Even in the haze of exhaustion, it still felt right.

As soon as we arrived, I went to bed and fell right asleep. My sister-in-law Donna, Jason's wife, was keeping me company in the other twin bed. I woke up suddenly in the middle of the night crying out, "Donna, I need to get Rebecca's yellow ribbons. She needs her ribbons!"

Rebecca had always been a thumb-sucker, especially when she was tired or just before she fell asleep. When she was little, she loved to rub the silky ribbon at the edge of her blanket while she sucked her thumb. Now all that was left of the blanket were two pieces of yellow ribbon. Like old friends, they gave her such comfort. She had even named them, Yelby and Lally. Before I left for Colorado we had hidden them together in her pillowcase so they would be there when she came home to my house.

"She needs her ribbons," I kept crying. Donna told me it was okay because she wouldn't need them in heaven. Once more, I realized she would never come home again. I didn't want to go home without her.

*　　*　　*

MAY 2020

I regret not spending time alone with Rebecca's body at the funeral home. I was in too much shock to understand how important this was, so I did not request it. I thank God for Sister Claire and her insistence that I see Rebecca. I needed that guidance. I wish someone, maybe the funeral director, had suggested that I stay behind or come back later and be alone with her. I could have talked to her, touched her, and kissed her one last time. I am thankful my mother thought to ask for some locks of her hair. I still touch them now and then. I also have a turquoise locket with her picture and a wisp of her hair. I wear it almost every day.

> "O Christ, that it were possible
> for one short hour to see
> The souls we loved, that they may tell us
> what and where they be."
> —ALFRED LORD TENNYSON

6
Faith

JUNE 2, 1994

Shining through the white ruffled curtains, the morning sun woke me. The spring day was inviting. As I squinted at the brightness, I remembered. I covered my head with the sheet, and wished that I was back in Colorado getting up for our hike in Estes Park. Instead, I had to prepare for Doug, Robin, and Rebecca's funeral. How unreal it all seemed.

Thoughts of Oliver got me up and took me downstairs to call the hospital. The nurse who answered the phone on 7 South told me Oliver had had a good night and was slowly improving. Momentarily relieved, I showered, ate, and dressed in a slow, mechanical manner. But I was grateful for my new dress. I made an effort to stand a little straighter. It was important for me to look good for Rebecca. I wanted her to be proud of me. I had always been so proud and happy to be her mother. Could this really be her last performance? How would I get through this day? How would I get through the days to come?

My mother's voice stopped my fearful thoughts. "We have to leave in a few minutes. The Mass is at eleven o'clock."

Shortly after arriving at the funeral home, I found out that Robin's family had decided to give her a separate funeral the next day in their home town of Lunenburg, located in the central part of the state. This change did not bother me. It made it easier just to focus on Doug and Rebecca. Robin needed her own day.

Our two large families gathered and filled the room. Doug's mom and her husband stood on one side of the room. Doug's dad and his wife were on the opposite side. His two brothers with their wives, and three of his four sisters had arrived from all over the country to be here. Added to this were my parents and my siblings. In the crowded room, the splendor and scent of all the flowers again mesmerized me. Doug's sister Kitty began giving each person a rose. As we left the funeral home, the roses seemed to unite our families in our grief.

There was a lot of confusion with cars and the procession. No one seemed to know what to do. My sister and I sat in the back seat of my father's Mercedes. It smelled, as always, faintly of cigars. Gripping the rose tighter, I looked out the car window at the royal-blue sky. There was not a cloud in sight. Silently, I said a prayer to Rebecca. "Honey, I need to know that you are okay. I need a rainbow over the church. Please."

As we approached the church, my mother almost shouted, "Look at the reporters!"

The accident continued to be in the national news, especially with the recent capture of the driver who had fled the scene. The cameras, news vans and enormous satellite dishes were lined up along the road in front of the church. They seemed so out of place, a cold harsh contrast to the budding trees and flowers behind them. I forgot my silent prayer.

My mother, father, and sister walked me down the aisle. I clutched my rose and clung to my mother's arm. I couldn't focus on anyone among the sea of faces looking intently at me. *Be not afraid, know that I am with you through it all,* sang the choir, and their soothing voices drew me along. As my mother guided me into the wooden pew, I noticed the rows and rows of silent, staring children—Rebecca's classmates and friends. They looked sad and confused. I felt the same way.

I watched the two caskets, surrounded by a group of Doug's friends, brought down the aisle toward the altar. I was surprised they were the same size. I had assumed Rebecca's would be smaller. I thought of her standing next to Doug, looking up at him adoringly. She had stood almost up to his chest. Again, I was comforted, knowing that they were together.

Father Tosti said the Mass and gave the sermon. Bits and pieces of his strong and reassuring message occasionally came through the thick mist of emotions swirling around me:

"Life is a gift from God, to be used, to be lived and then to change. Death will come inevitably to all of us. When it comes swiftly and unannounced and to the young, if we have faith and believe when Death comes, it is not all over. It is only a beginning. Children must ask what happens now. Death is not a stone wall that has no gates. A gate opens on that wall into a beautiful new life, more wonderful than this one."

I could picture the three of them in this new place he was describing. I wondered if they could see us. I didn't think Doug would like the big church service. He probably would have liked something simple by the ocean. The 1,000-seat capacity church was filled to overflowing. *But we needed this huge church to fit all these people*, I argued with him in my mind.

"God can do better than we can." Father Tosti's voice penetrated the fog once more.

This sounded right, but my heart insisted Rebecca needed her mother. And I needed my little girl. My ears were plugged, as if I had just come up from underwater to get air.

His muffled voice continued on. "Life is fragile, like a crystal vase, to be held gently and carefully."

An image of a shattered vase came into my head. Was it my fault? Had I not been careful enough? I only knew I wanted to hold my little girl. Was she really over there in that box?

Through the rest of the Mass, I rose, knelt, and recited prayers by rote motion. The white robes of the priests and the gentle clanging of the incense burners as they swung them over the coffins gave me a feeling of being in another place, another time, the acrid smell and smoke from the burning incense drugging me. As the choir sang *On Eagle's Wings* I drifted off, momentarily soaring with the eagle, escaping into other realms. In a stupor, I watched all the people and children going to communion. Were there so many Catholics here?

Then it was time for Margo to give the eulogy for Doug.

"Doug was a Cape Codder. He thought it was the best place to be," she began, her voice strong and clear.

"Handsome, talented, charming"—I could feel her warmth and love, and the pride she had for her son. "Even when things weren't going well, he always said Rebecca and Ollie are great!" Yes, I agreed, he loved them so much. She ended by reading a poem Doug had written this past Christmas.

I can't get the cards out on time, not this year,
and I can't seem to shop at the mall.
Seems like it was only a few days ago,
that we saw the beginning of fall.

What is it, I ponder as I rake up my leaves,
and roll up the volleyball net.
That makes me bewildered, that makes me believe,
that Christmastime isn't here yet?

A day off would help, I admit to myself,
as I store the grill inside the shed.
And I look at the hole that I dug in the ground,
for Oliver's basketball net.

Did I do anything this year? I chided myself
as I was fixing Rebecca's flat tire.
Anything at all I can tell my friends,
without sounding a bit like a liar?

The air conditioner seems a bit more heavy this year,
I tell Rob as I haul it inside.
Oh it can't be the end of the year quite so soon,
No it can't be December, I cried.

As I took in my bathing suit from out on the line,
I thought of what I might have done.
Stories that I might have written to share.
Elections that I might have won.

Oh what glorious achievements I'd have,
to reminisce on now and to boast.
What a modern-day 90s success I would be,
If I'd only done half what I hoped.

But the feet float up high in my Lazy Boy chair,
And the kids get all cozy as they join me there.
Now who could leave this to go shopping, and why,
When they've still got flags up from the Fourth of July?

So we've settled in nice,
and we'll wait for the spirit,
and we'll listen in wonder,
and you know, when we hear it?

We'll know in our hearts it was right,
to just stop,
And tell someone you love 'em
That you love 'em a lot.

His words touched my heart. It was almost as if he knew. Oh Doug, we need you.

I didn't know Tara was giving the eulogy for Rebecca. As my sister walked towards the podium, the lump in my throat grew larger. I fought back tears. I was amazed that she could do this. Public speaking was something we both avoided. Tentatively, Tara adjusted the microphone. Her notes rustled in her trembling hands. She cleared her throat.

"I'm not very good at standing in front of an audience and speaking, but Rebecca was great at it. So, I've asked her to come here today and help me out."

I thought how much Rebecca loved to be on stage. I remembered that today would have been the day of her sixth-grade school play. She had rehearsed her role as a nerd for months and couldn't wait to make everyone laugh. I planned to braid her hair and make it stand on end by putting a wire in it, like Pippi Longstocking's.

Breathing deeply, I thought how strange it was to be at her funeral instead.

"I was with Terece and Doug the day Rebecca was born," Tara continued.

Suddenly I was at Rebecca's birth, Tara and I chanting and breathing together as one. The incredible feeling of birthing my first child and holding Rebecca in my arms came right back.

Tara's voice was enchanting. I hung on every word, grasping for Rebecca's life in her words. She talked of images of Rebecca that she kept getting during these past difficult days. One was of Rebecca, just before her fourth birthday, dancing at our brother John and Carol's wedding.

"She had her dance partner all picked out, a slightly older man, her then six-year-old cousin Seth—two little blond children holding one another and doing their version of the waltz."

Closing my eyes, I saw Rebecca perfectly, all dressed up in her dark blue ruffled sundress with tiny white flowers, gazing adoringly at Seth, handsome in his navy-blue blazer. Tara's voice came drifting into my vision.

"Rebecca was having such a wonderful time dancing, acting so grown up with a big smile on her face, that even though she really, really had to go to the bathroom, she didn't want to leave the dance floor. And so, she didn't."

I smiled and saw clearly the puddle on the floor. Rebecca ignored it completely, waiting for the next song.

Tara spoke of Rebecca's "energy, zeal, and enthusiasm for life. Rebecca put her whole heart into everything she did, practicing for the school play, dancing, drawing, writing her poetry, or just playing with her many friends."

I leaned forward, wanting to absorb the words that were bringing Rebecca back to me. I could see her and feel the joy she had given me.

Tara ended with, "The final memory of Rebecca is of her beautiful long, blond hair, like a princess in a fairy tale. And I see that little princess walking in the garden of the Lord, Doug and Robin each holding a hand. But Rebecca, because we do love you so much, honey, we are really, really going to miss you."

Don't stop! I wanted to shout. As Tara talked, Rebecca was still with me. As she came back from the altar, I was slowly losing the images and falling back into the dense fog that seemed to surround and protect me.

And then I heard someone singing. I thought it was Mariah Carey herself. My heart skipped a beat. She sang about the sorrow and going deep inside and finding your inner strength, the hero in you.

I sat spellbound as the melodious voice continued, singing about hope and the promise of tomorrow.

The words haunted me. Rebecca had sung them to me so many times in the previous weeks. It was almost as if on some deep soul level, she knew she was leaving and was trying to prepare me. Could that be? Why didn't I know? Did God need her for something? But I needed her, too.

How could I go on without her, my sweet, amazing child? Tears rolled down my cheeks as she sang the last line about finding your way. I had to believe that. Hope was all I had.

The Mass was over. I felt my parents' arms in mine, guiding me out. The lilting sound of the choir as they sang *We Remember Them* moved me along. We followed the crowd to the parish hall where refreshments would be served. Before going inside, I thought of the rainbow and looked up. The sky was clear, blue, and empty. Disappointed, I went into the hall. Tara was the first to approach me.

"Terece, I have to tell you about a dream I had last night. I dreamt there was a beautiful rainbow over the church."

My eyes opened wide as my heart leapt.

"Oh my God, that's my rainbow! I prayed to Rebecca for a rainbow over the church!"

I hugged her, satisfied. My prayer had been answered. Feeling stronger, I turned to face the crowd. A young couple came up to me first.

"I don't know if you remember us. We are friends of Doug from his work. He was our videographer. We want to tell you about an incredible rainbow we saw last night on the way to the wake. We felt like it was Doug having a field day up there with his own audio-visual equipment. The rainbow was like special effects for a movie."

Shocked, I told them about my prayer. Before they could respond, another friend came up to us and told about seeing a beautiful rainbow over the scene of the accident as they were driving from Boston to the funeral that day. Then someone else told me about a rainbow they had seen near the funeral home during the previous night's wake.

Their stories uplifted me and made me want to escape into the images of the rainbows and the feeling that maybe Rebecca was okay. I stood away from the crowd, not wanting to face them all again. Friends brought me food, but I couldn't eat. Faces became blurry, and I was relieved when my parents came and drove me back to their house.

In Cotuit, my family gathered again. I was in a hurry to get back to the hospital. I pushed the sadness of the day away and focused on Oliver. I was impatient to be alone. Jane arrived to drive me back to Boston. We stopped to get Christy, who had come from Colorado for the funeral, to give her a ride to the airport. As we left town, I thought of the last drive with Christy to the airport in Denver. Although only five days had passed, it felt like years ago, another lifetime. I stared vacantly out the window again. Suddenly, the sky ahead filled with color. Realizing what it was, I screamed, "Stop the car! It's a rainbow! A real rainbow!"

The beauty and richness of the colors took my breath away. Red, orange, yellow, blue, green, and purple bands blended into one magnificent ray that seemed to come straight from heaven. I no longer had any doubt. I whispered silently, *Thank you, God. Thank you, Rebecca.*

Elated, I babbled most of the way to Boston. I told them how Rebecca had always painted and drawn rainbows since she was a little girl. She drew them on Mother's Day cards, valentines, letters, and papers she brought home from school.

When I arrived at the hospital, a smiling nurse handed me a message from Tara. The note read, "Terece, Rebecca's rainbow was here in Cotuit. Out over the ocean, it was beautiful." I closed my eyes. I felt warmth and light beginning to maybe heal a little my broken heart.

*   *   *

MAY 2020

The miracle of Rebecca's rainbow will always be with me. Every time I see one, I think of her as saying, *Hello, I love you, keep on keeping on, everything will be all right.* My family and friends always send me pictures whenever a rainbow appears to them, often around her birthday, August 18, and the anniversary of her death, May 28. It's one way she shares her love and God's love. She reminds us we are all connected.

The rainbow seemed like the first step in my healing journey, which I know now will continue for my lifetime. Coming up this month on the twenty-sixth anniversary, I see that the messages—the roses, the coins, the songs, and the rainbows—were just a beginning. They gave me hope, but more than that they strengthened my Faith. Faith that a power greater than we can ever imagine is at work here. Trust in that power. We don't know God's plan.

"Faith is a knowledge within the heart,
beyond the reach of proof."

—Kahil Gibran

Rebecca and me — July 1983

Rebecca and me — September 1984

Rebecca and Doug — July 1986

Rebecca and Doug — August 1990

Rebecca — April 1991

7
Pain

The sterile, gray, and quiet of the hospital halls felt better to me than the busy outside world bursting with the cheerfulness of spring. The confinement made me feel safe, like being at home with the shades drawn when you want to keep the world out. I was relieved and glad to see Oliver. As we hugged, I thought how good it was to touch him. He smiled at me and wiggled around in his bed as much as he could with his leg suspended in traction. Jane gave Oliver his favorite blue blanket that she had picked up at my house. His eyes lit up as he snuggled into the familiar softness. At nine years old he still found comfort in it. Jane stayed with Oliver as I walked Stacy to the elevator to say good-bye.

"Thanks so much for being with him. I don't know how I would have made it through the funeral if I had to worry about him. I'm sorry you couldn't be there. It was beautiful, but so sad. Still doesn't seem real."

Stacy replied, "I would rather have been here with Oliver—I hate funerals." Handing me a notebook, she continued,

"These are notes that Nathaniel's parents and I wrote about everything that happened while you were gone. He slept on and off most of the time, watching parts of a movie and even playing a little Nintendo. His legs were itchy, so the nurse gave him an alcohol rub. They also took him off morphine and changed it to Tylex."

She looked at me hesitantly. "Oliver asked me a lot of questions. He kept asking me what day it was. Then he said, 'Stacy, Dad died and Rebecca died and Robin died,' and before I could answer, he asked me if they really died. I told him they did, and we cried together. He asked me the same thing at least four times. Then he would sleep."

She took a deep breath and went on. "He also asked me, 'Who will I stay with at Dad's house when I stay there now?' I told him he would stay with you all the time now and that he wouldn't stay at his Dad's house anymore. He got upset and said, 'But that is not the way we do it. We go to Dad's house, too.' I just told him things would be a little different now, but that I loved him very much and I would always be with him. He smiled and fell back asleep."

We cried and hugged. I thanked her again and said I was glad Oliver could talk to her. "He always puts on a brave face for me, like he's trying to protect me." It was so hard for us as adults to understand, but so much harder for a child.

We said good-bye, and I sat in the lounge for a minute, alone with my thoughts. I was so grateful for my family and friends who seemed to be holding me together. Slowly, I walked back to the room.

The next two days passed. Oliver's medical progress was amazing. The bruises faded and he slept less. Balloons and cards were all over the room. He even had a visit from a pink Power Ranger. I clung to the routines of the hospital to steady me.

JUNE 4, 1994

I had to go back to the Cape again for the burial on Saturday, June 4, 1994. June 4 was Rebecca's best friend's twelfth birthday. It would be the first birthday of Meghan's life that Rebecca would miss. Her mom, Jackie, and I had been pregnant together. The girls had been friends since infancy. They brought out the best in each other, and with their blonde hair and blue eyes, they looked and acted like sisters. They each wore matching halves of a heart, a best friend's necklace; how difficult for Meghan to turn twelve that day and know that Rebecca never would.

The burial was at the Marstons Mills cemetery. Standing in the sunshine, I thought of Meghan and wished we were all together at her birthday party. Doug's mom and her husband had chosen a beautiful spot under a large oak tree in the far right corner of the small cemetery. It was private and peaceful. Although Doug and Rebecca had been cremated, their ashes were buried along with Robin's body. Father Tosti and Robin's stepfather both said prayers and spoke. Then it was time to say good-bye to them. It had been a long week.

After the burial, Robin's family invited everyone to lunch at the same venue in Osterville where Doug and Robin had celebrated their marriage only six months ago. I thought how sad and difficult it must be for them. I didn't go. I just wanted to get back to the hospital.

On Sunday, Oliver's friend Chunukee and his family came to visit. Their strong presence meant so much to me. Knowing that people cared so deeply and wanted to help gripped my heart. Tara and her family came to visit, too. Tentative at first, his cousins gradually relaxed to Oliver's welcome smile. They brought some string cream and sprayed it all over the room, much to Oliver's delight. Doug's relatives streamed through to say good-bye on their way back to their homes in Seattle, St. Paul, Albuquerque, and Scottsdale.

A few days passed. The doctors told me they had to put Oliver in a spica cast to stabilize his hips before he could go home. They explained this cast would go from under his arms to his ankle with only the right leg free. Up until now his leg had been in traction, but he could wiggle and move around a little. My brother John and his wife, Carol, came to be with us for this procedure. Oliver had to be put under anesthesia.

Sitting in the waiting room, I heard Oliver screaming. He had woken up terrified and unable to move.

"Please go be with him! I can't!" I cried out to John and Carol. I ran from the room, unable to bear his pain.

Away from the screams, I stood in the corridor shaking and crying. I wondered if he was having flashbacks. All I could imagine was the horror he must have felt being crushed and trapped in that car. I felt so helpless. I couldn't stop crying. Finally, Carol came out and told me that because Oliver was so hysterical, the doctors agreed to cut the cast down a couple inches so it wouldn't cover his chest as much. It made him feel like he was suffocating. John was calming him down.

John's confident and authoritative manner was so like Doug's, I knew it would help Oliver relax. They finally wheeled him out. He had stopped screaming, but he looked so scared. John and Carol kept talking to him in soothing voices. I just held his hand and fought back my tears. How could an active nine-year-old stand not being able to move? How much more could we handle? He was calmer when we got back to his room. The cast was a bright green, and we teased him and said that he looked like a Ninja turtle. He even smiled.

He slowly adjusted to the spica cast and finally, on June 9, Oliver was ready to be discharged from the hospital and go home. And that meant I had to go home too.

$$\star \quad \star \quad \star$$

MAY 2020

One of the most heartbreaking experiences as a parent is to see your child in pain and suffering. I felt so helpless and frightened, and yet I had to be strong and brave to comfort Oliver and convince him that he would be okay. Again, I am so grateful to those who took over when I couldn't bear it or couldn't be there with him. A presence, big and powerful, seemed to surround us. For me it was God, expressing through the hands and hearts of my family, friends, and strangers. I believe the power of prayer helped Oliver's recovery to go quickly and well. The accident touched so many families, and because of the publicity, people were praying all over the country. I received many letters and cards to verify that. Never underestimate the power of prayer.

Together, Oliver and I were just beginning our journey of healing that would continue to this day. His teenage years and early twenties were especially difficult as he struggled with depression, survivor guilt, and loss. Often, when I had no control over a situation, I would pray and put him in God's hands. And in God's hands is love. That's all that really matters.

When Oliver turned 18, and could get a tattoo without my permission, he designed one to cover his back: *In God's Hands, Rest in Peace Dad, Robin and Becky.* When he went to have it done, the tattoo artist could not do it all in one session. So across his shoulders, it says *In God's Hands.* He never did finish the rest of it. It gives me comfort, even if I'm not a big tattoo fan.

Healing takes time and lots of love. I've learned that your heart can handle so much more than you can ever imagine.

"Prayer is putting oneself in the
Hands of God."

—Mother Teresa

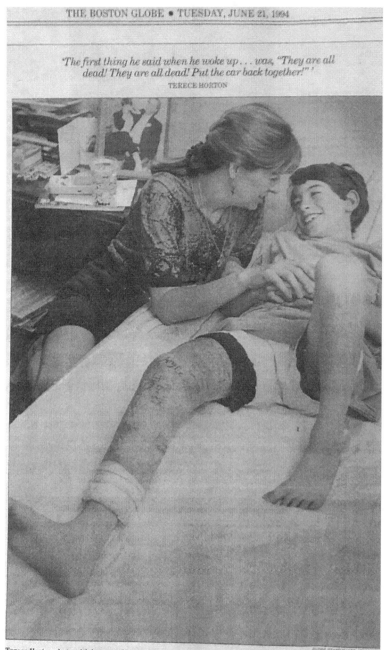

'The first thing he said when he woke up . . . was, "They are all dead! They are all dead! Put the car back together!"'

TERECE HORTON

GLOBE STAFF PHOTO / TOM HER

Terece Horton chats with her son, Oliver, 9, at their Marstons Mills home yesterday. Oliver, the only survivor of Route 3 collision that killed his sister, father and stepmother, is expected to recover fully from his injuries.

Oliver and me — Boston Globe June 1994

8
Home

It was time for Oliver and me to leave the safety and confines of the hospital and go back into the world. Nothing would ever be the same again. My life was now divided in two parts, Before and After the accident.

We were all concerned that Oliver would have trouble getting back into a vehicle. My brothers rode with him in the ambulance from Boston to our home in Marstons Mills. I went ahead with Suzanne in her car. As we pulled in the driveway, I was amazed. Out of loving hearts and the desire to help, my wonderful friends and family had transformed my home. Outside, leaves had been raked, a brick walk had been built and lined with pink impatiens, roses had been planted, and a beautiful statue of a child surrounded by animals sat under a new rhododendron bush. It was so welcoming, I didn't have a chance to feel apprehensive.

Inside, my living room had been made into a hospital room with two beds, towels, and a wash basin. Oliver's get-well cards were hung on the walls, and a picture of him and his dad had been placed by his bed. In the kitchen, the shelves were filled with food. Jane and Mary and a few other close friends were there to greet us. Tears welled up again and I lost my voice. I was finally home.

When I could, I thanked everyone for their help. I had been feeling so overwhelmed, I had not even thought about food or what I would need. Then a car pulled in the driveway. My first thought was it must be Doug and Rebecca in Doug's little blue Ford Fiesta. I could picture the two of them smiling and talking away, and Rebecca, jumping out of the car, happy to see me with news to report and a pretty card or picture she had made for me.

"It's the ambulance with Oliver," Mary said, bringing me back to the moment.

We went out to greet him. As soon as he saw me, Oliver became agitated and upset.

"He's been fine the whole trip," John reassured me. "Let's get him inside."

John carried him into his bed. Oliver liked the fact that we would be staying together in the living room. Slowly, everyone began to leave so we could settle in. I asked someone to go upstairs and close the door to Rebecca's room. I could not face it yet.

Stacy stayed with us that first night. We all slept in the living room, Stacy on the couch and Oliver and I in the beds. I worried about Oliver falling out of bed so we put pillows on the floor. At one point, Stacy woke and caught him just as he started falling.

In the middle of the night, Oliver screamed. It was a terrifying sound. Although he was yelling and screaming, he seemed to be asleep. We couldn't wake him. I had never witnessed night terrors before. I felt scared and almost paralyzed seeing him so out of control. Thank goodness, Stacy was calm and steady. Finally, he drifted into a quieter sleep. But it was a long time before I fell asleep. I wondered how I was going to deal with his emotional state. How long would the night screaming go on? Why had this happened? Everything was so different; even my house didn't feel or look the same. I felt so afraid and alone. Doug had always handled any kind of crisis we faced. But now it was all up to me.

The next morning a VNA nurse came to monitor Oliver's care. I knew Yvonne from my work in health care. Her English accent and pleasant, competent manner put us all at ease. She explained how to wean Oliver off the Adivan. The drug kept him in a fog. I wanted my Oliver back.

Later that day, a physical therapist from the VNA arrived to help work with Oliver's muscles while he was in the spica cast. An older woman with a very efficient manner, she got right to work without developing any kind of rapport with either of us. Oliver grimaced as she briskly started to move his leg. He looked over to me with a "help me" expression. It hit me how fragile we were. It was as though we were standing on thin ice; any wrong move and we would fall through. I tried to explain that this young boy was dealing with much more than a broken hip.

"What do I do?" I asked Stacy after a second session that didn't go well. "I hate confrontations, but she is just not working out."

Without waiting for a reply, I ran out and caught her in the driveway.

"This isn't working. Oliver's emotional state can't handle your demands."

"But . . . I have my agenda to follow," she argued.

"I'm sorry, but I have to ask you not to come back," I said firmly. She left.

The uncomfortable discussion was over. Breathing deeply, I stood quietly in the soft sunshine of the June morning. The strength had come from somewhere, like the invisible roots that nourished the sturdy oak tree in my back yard.

Later, after a call to the VNA, a new physical therapist was sent to us. A delight from the start, Brenda had a daughter named Rebecca, who was in third grade with Oliver. Oliver enjoyed her visits and worked hard with her.

My family and friends had agreed to take turns staying with Oliver and me at night. But after that first night, Stacy was ready to move in.

"I'll stay until I go back to Wheelock in the fall. I've told Camp Lyndon I won't be able to work there this summer."

"But you were going to be the director." I started to argue and then stopped. "I do need you," I told her, thinking of all the love she had given Rebecca and Oliver since they were babies. I knew she needed to stay, too. Stacy had lost her own mother to leukemia when she was eleven years old, the same age as Rebecca. She understood our grief.

A couple days later, I was sitting outside on my porch alone. The mail lady stopped across the street. Instead of putting the mail in my box, she got out and walked toward me with a large stack of cards. She approached slowly, as if uncertain of my reaction. I felt as if I had a condition that might be contagious. Her pity engulfed me like a wave washing over a shell sticking out of the sand.

"Thank you," I said, taking the cards from her. Would people ever know how to act around me again?

The stack of cards became a daily ritual. The amount that arrived was astonishing, some from complete strangers. I never knew there were so many sympathy cards. I seldom got any duplicates. All were words of comfort, sorrow, peace, and hope. One day I received a letter from a woman who explained that she had lost her two sons, ages 21 and 23, when their snowmobile sunk though the ice. I was horrified. Both children! She told me about her pain and her long grief process. But what she wanted me to know is that she is surviving, finding her way. I clung to that hope. How long would it take me to find my way?

The outside world seemed so far away. I didn't want visitors. I didn't want to have to talk to anyone. All my effort went to taking care of Oliver. As the hospital had, our home became a sanctuary for us. As difficult as it was for Oliver to be in the spica cast, for me he seemed safe in it, contained. I was so afraid of anything more happening to him. I wanted him to be protected. Stacy answered the phone and met people at the door to explain my need to be alone. A huge help was the food that friends and family dropped off—lasagna, fruit bowls, brownies, cookies, carrot juice, and much more. I'm sure I would not have eaten much otherwise.

Jane gave me two books about mothers who had lost children. She knew that when I wanted to learn about something, I read every book I could find on the subject. *Lessons of Love* by Melodie Beattie became my bible. Melodie had lost her son, Shane, in a freak skiing accident. She was a single mother with a son and a daughter, like me. Shane was just twelve when he died. I could relate to her so much. Her shared experience helped me face my life. Paula D'Arcy's book, *Song for Sarah*, touched me deeply. Our situations were so similar. Her husband and eighteen-month-old daughter, Sarah, had been killed by a drunk driver. She and her unborn baby survived the crash. I felt a connection to both of these women whom I had never met. It was easier to read about their lives than face mine.

I deliberately avoided thinking about Rebecca. It was too difficult. Whenever thoughts would come, I pushed them away. But one morning, I decided to try to face my grief.

"I'm going upstairs to my room," I told Stacy. "I need to cry."

Alone, playing *Hero* on my cassette player, I sat on the rug with my arms wrapped around my knees. The song tore at my heart and the tears began to flow. My sobbing grew louder and louder, coming from somewhere inside I'd never been before. It frightened me, and I was afraid Oliver might hear. I didn't want to scare him. So, I stopped, pushing back down that horrible pain. After washing my face, I went back downstairs. Oliver stared at me with a sad look.

I forced a smile. "I'm okay," I said.

It was the arrival of the wheelchair that helped connect us back to the outside world beyond the house. Because of the body cast that encased him from under his arms to the ankle of one leg, Oliver had to be almost flat in the chair. As soon as he adjusted to it, he wanted us to take him for a walk in the neighborhood. He loved being outside again. We all did. Birds singing, gentle breezes, and the sparkling water of the nearby Shubael Pond greeted us as Stacy and I pushed Oliver along. I wondered what people were thinking—the bright green body cast, the extended wheelchair and the strange noises Oliver made at intervals, like the cries of a wounded animal. He had been making these same loud sounds when he played Nintendo from his bed. Even stranger was that he never looked distressed as he made these noises. They just seemed to come out of him.

When Oliver was a baby, he smiled all the time but made no sounds at all until he was almost two years old. Even with speech therapy, his words were undistinguishable until he started kindergarten. Although he was always on the quiet side, once he started reading, his speech was fine.

Now it seemed that these primitive sounds were releasing some of the horror out of his body. I think it was helpful for him. He seemed to be able to release where I couldn't. If only I could just let it go, instead of planning it.

One afternoon, Oliver was in the backyard with Brenda, the physical therapist, learning to walk with crutches. Stacy had gone to her dad's house to get some clothes and other things. When the phone rang, I answered it.

"Good afternoon! This is Cambridge Eye calling to let you know Rebecca's glasses are in and ready to be picked up."

My breath caught in my throat. I remembered those glasses. We had ordered them right before I left for Colorado and had fun picking them out together. Rebecca was so excited she was going to try transition lenses that would turn into sunglasses when she went outside. Her blue eyes were sensitive, and I thought she would need them when Doug took Robin and the kids to a big Horton family reunion at a dude ranch in Colorado in July. Now they were ready to be picked up.

"Sorry," I told the lady. "Rebecca died."

"Oh," she replied, then was speechless.

I tried to tell myself that she wouldn't need glasses in heaven. But I wanted her to have those glasses. I wanted her back. We never had much money for extras and Rebecca was so happy with anything new. I wanted to see her face when she put them on. Please come home, Rebecca. Your glasses are ready.

*   *   *

MAY 29, 2020

As I write this today, on the twenty-sixth anniversary, I am filled with gratitude. Rebecca was such a gift to my life. Her love is still here and is stronger than ever, reaching and touching so many hearts. This chapter is evidence of all the love and support that enabled us to go on, one moment to one step, to one day, one week, one month, and now twenty-six years.

Coming home without Rebecca was almost unbearable. I am so grateful to my family and friends who transformed my home, but left Rebecca's room waiting for me until I was ready. It was a while before I could open that door, but I did.

I will be forever grateful that Stacy stayed and was with us that summer to grieve, heal, and learn to live again in a new way. Giving up her summer job as the Director of Camp Lyndon was a big decision to make, especially in light of her plan to become a teacher. Stacy helped soften the pain and filled the empty parts of us by playing many roles—sister, father, daughter, and dear friend. We often laughed about her many hats. Her presence was calming and confident. We needed that. Although she went back to Wheelock in the fall, she continued to live with us weekends and full-time after graduation for six more years as she began her teaching career. She is family to me and has been there for us to this day, in so many ways. She was heaven-sent. Thank you, Stacy.

"The wound is the place where the light enters you."

—RUMI

Rebecca, Stacy, and Oliver — Christmas 1993

9
Strength

I had to pick a stone out for Rebecca's grave. My mother came to drive me. I still could not get behind the wheel of a car.

Again, I was in a foreign world, walking around monuments and gravestones. They seemed like strangers, silent and staring. What would I engrave? How could I say all I wanted in a few words? How could I put my love on such a cold, hard surface? It seemed so final. I decided quickly so we could leave that place. After choosing a flat, gray stone with flowers along the edges, I wrote on the order form:

REBECCA T. HORTON

"BECKY"

AUGUST 18, 1982 - MAY 29, 1994

WE LOVE YOU

My body rigid, I sat in silence on the way home. I kept thinking it wasn't enough. How could that marker represent Rebecca's shining light? I had no answers.

The following day, my mother came to pick me up again. Her love, grief, and concern guided me on. She took me to see Henry, a therapist I had seen during my divorce. His kindness and wisdom comforted me. On a spiritual level, I could grasp some of what had happened. Talking with Henry helped strengthen my belief that Rebecca had a greater mission beyond this life. My faith in God and the Divine Plan was strong.

"I know we will always be connected and I will see her again when I die," I told him, trying to convince myself. This belief gave some life back to my paralyzed form. It made death not seem so final. This was the only explanation that made sense. I would see them all again. I would just have to be patient. I clung to that hope like a drowning woman in a stormy sea grabbing a rope that's thrown to her.

Oliver also had a therapist come to see him at the house, a man he had seen for a while during the divorce, also. One of the things they did was draw pictures. Oliver made a picture of himself in the green spica cast.

"Look, Mom," he said, "I drew me mad and sad." Jerry also helped him talk about his dad, and they made a card for him in heaven for Father's Day. Oliver could only focus on his dad. It was too much to try to think about Rebecca and Robin, too. He never mentioned their names.

On Father's Day, Oliver wanted to go to the cemetery. He had missed the wake, funerals, and burial, and needed to see the graves. He needed a place to take his card. I had finally started to drive again, but I was still wary of cars. They had betrayed me.

"I'll drive you," I told Oliver, wondering if he would be able to get in a car again. Stacy and I put the seat back so he could ride flat since his body did not bend with the cast. We helped him out on his crutches and he just did it, and got in the car without saying a word. I let my breath out slowly. His quiet strength and courage amazed and led me.

After three weeks of being confined to the neighborhood, he was glad to be out in the world again. He did better than I did at the cemetery. The three graves surrounded by flowers under the big oak tree made it feel like a private sanctuary. The summer sun shined softly and the birds greeted us with their chatter. Oliver left the Father's Day card he had made. "Dear Daddy, I hope you are happy in Heaven but I wish you were here with me."

Tears flowing down my cheeks, I wondered how much my heart could take. It was bad enough for my own heart to break, but to see my little boy's pain was much worse. And so, we left. On the way home, we stopped at the nearby video store. Since Oliver was so physically restricted, Nintendo filled a lot of his day. The owner of the store kindly gave us free games and movies. His compassion and generosity helped ease our grief a little. Thank you, Jimmy.

During those first few weeks at home, as I was focused on Oliver and our immediate needs, life was proceeding around us. There were things that needed taking care of.

"Margo's here," Stacy announced, as Doug's mom came through the door. After hugs and a visit with Oliver, we sat and talked.

"We have to sell Doug's house immediately because of the high mortgage," she said softly. I could hear the wisdom in her words, and I hoped she would stay a while longer before going back to Albuquerque.

"We will have to clean it out first. Bill and your Mom and Dad are helping."

I thought about Bill, Doug's dad. A serious, kind, and intelligent man, Bill and his new wife, Lois, lived in Phoenix. Doug and his dad had similar qualities, although Doug was more carefree and fun-loving. He could never have imagined his parents having to undertake this task. Neither could I.

I nodded at Margo. We looked at each other, still not believing, holding our emotions back like a sea wall stopping the crashing waves. After she left, I thought about Doug's house. When we separated, he didn't want to be far from Rebecca and Oliver, so he bought an old house about two miles from us on the other side of Shubael Pond. It needed a lot of work, and as he did with everything, he put all his energy into fixing it up. I pictured it now— dishes piled up in the sink, clothes strung about, Harry the bird on his perch in the picture window, Rebecca's homework scattered over the kitchen table, letters that needed answers, music waiting to be played, food to be cooked, Robin's flowers needing water. How could no one be coming home? I pushed the images out of my mind. I had to.

The next day, boxes of things from Doug's house began

arriving. They were all marked: *Rebecca's Clothes, Doug's Clothes, Sheets, Doug's CD's*. I put them all in my spare room without opening any of them. The piles grew over the next few days. It seemed strange, almost as if Doug were moving back in. But where was he? All these reminders and memories sitting there, waiting . . . for what?

$$\star \quad \star \quad \star$$

JUNE 2020

As I rewrite this, I realize how incredibly difficult this had to be for my mother and father. As I could not bear to see Oliver in pain, they were experiencing the same feelings for me, their daughter. They had also lost a granddaughter. All I saw at the time was how strong and kind they were, doing whatever they could to help. I gained strength from their love. My mom helped so much with the funeral, picking out the gravestone, driving me to appointments and praying. They both helped with the cleaning out and selling of Doug's house. For many years to come, my Dad would come over and work in my yard, picking up sticks, weeding, and mowing my lawn. He never said much, but his quiet presence outside felt as if he was guarding and watching over us. My Dad died fourteen years later after suffering with Alzheimer's for six years. I sometimes wonder if it was all too much for him. I am so grateful and blessed to have had such love in my life.

I also see and understand how deeply my sister, Tara, was affected by the accident. The morning the police arrived on her doorstep looking for me, she had been lying awake with her hands on her stomach, knowing and acknowledging she was pregnant again. At forty-two, with a nine-, a fourteen- and a sixteen-year-old, this was a surprise that filled her with joy. And then there was a knock on the front door. A police officer and a distraught Jane stood on the doorstep. Tara had to make that call to me, to be the messenger of devastating news she knew could destroy me. Her husband then drove her to Boston to be with Oliver and stayed with him until I arrived. She delivered a beautiful, heartbreaking, but uplifting eulogy. She loved and supported me. She loved Rebecca dearly and had to process that loss, too. The whole time she had this secret she was carrying inside her. How could she share it with me? I had lost a daughter and she was having a baby. I don't know how she did it. Her inner strength, love, and devotion felt like an infusion from God. Thank you, Tara. When she finally told me a month later, I could not understand why God was giving her another child and taking mine. It seemed so unfair, and this was very hard for both of us. But love got us through.

Six months later she gave birth a month early to Samuel, a wonderful addition to our family.

> "It's the Circle of Life and it moves us all,
> through despair and hope, through faith and love,
> 'til we find our place on the path unwinding."
> —ELTON JOHN

10
Friendship

JUNE 23, 1994

School was ending for the summer. Oliver's third-grade teacher and the principal of the Marstons Mills Elementary school that he had attended came to visit. They brought with them Get Well and Sympathy cards from the whole school.

"Look Mom, this one is from Nate," he smiled, pleased with all the attention.

The visit seemed to help him remember. It gave him a connection with his friends and classmates, like a hand reaching out and bringing him back to his life and the world. But it was not a place he could stay in for long. It was almost too much to let it in. Then we would have to believe it, that Doug and Rebecca were really gone. I still felt as if we were going through the motions, getting by, until they came home again.

Rebecca had attended the sixth-grade school, a separate building in Hyannis. Her teachers invited me there to a tree planting ceremony in Rebecca's memory. I stood with all of Rebecca's friends, classmates, and teachers, and again I felt removed, as if an observer to a play I didn't understand. I threw a shovel of dirt in the hole and thanked them. Her homeroom teacher gave me a box with her work and letters that the children had written. Later that day I sat and read about death from a twelve-year-old's perspective. Some of the letters were for me, but most of them were addressed "Dear Becky."

The whole class is feeling bad now that you're gone, but you have gone to a better place. You've been taken because you were needed. Everyone misses you very much. You and your spirit is all around us. Thank you for all you have done for us. You are still in our hearts always.

We will love her beautiful smile always.
 Monique

Hi, it's me Sam. How are things up there? Everything is fine here. If you can read this letter, will you try to talk to me or communicate with me. Did you see Elvis! I hope everything is ok. We all miss you very much. When I die, you have to promise to meet me somewhere, like at the Pearly Gates or something.

She was always kind to everyone even if they were
mean to her.

    Samantha

For Becky Horton - a soul that touched everyone
– did she ever know that's she's my hero – she's
everything I wish I could be. I can fly higher than an
eagle for Becky is the wind beneath my wings.

    Nikki

Beckie is always with you where ever you go. Beckie
always lived life to the fullest. It makes me want to
enjoy life a little more and live each day to the fullest.

    Tiffany

I think she reflected how life should be. Nobody
complain or being mean to anyone else, or judging
people by their past or background. I just can't say
how much I admired her determination and the
respect she had for everybody's feelings.

    Anna

I'm sorry I made fun of you pitching so bad. I'm glad for all the good things I said to you before you died.

    Greg

I wish I could take back all the mean things I said to you but it is too late now for that so this is my way to say sorry. I hope you can forgive me.
You never know how nice someone is until they are gone, then it's too late.

    Geoff

May a golden tear from Heaven above guide you through this sorrow.

    Amber

She was always bright and cheerful. She made the whole class bright and cheerful when we were down. She was a great student and wonderful friend. I will always remember her. She was a true friend.

    Stephanie

* * *

JUNE 2020

The letters were sweet and sad reflections of thoughts on life. I realized how full Rebecca's life had been outside of home and how many children she had touched. I wished she could have been in the school play. She was dedicated and had practiced so long for it. At the tree ceremony, her art teacher gave me a letter:

Your daughter was EXTREMELY talented. As the author of

the school play, I was present at the auditions. Over 130

kids tried out. I used a rating system of 1-5 points. She was

the only child that I gave a 5-plus to. She just transformed

herself when she got on stage, and I told her that afterwards.

Rebecca was a wonderful actress and a great kid.

She was allowed to pick whatever part she wanted. I remember her bringing home the script and choosing the part with the most lines. She loved performing and shined on stage. She really did seize every moment. Is that what life is about? But if she was such a good example, why did she die? We need her. We need her kindness, her cheerfulness, her brightness. Please God, why her?

No one is ever prepared for tragedy. When children lose

a friend, a brother or a sister, they want to know why, too. What do you say? You want to find words to satisfy them but will make sense to yourself, too. Rebecca's friends had so many questions. Meghan asked me, "What happened to her braces when she died?" Oliver struggled to understand, too. He had lost so much.

Children all react differently. The world of imagination can be more real to them than the observable one. But children can simplify that which we as adults can make more complicated. Sometimes "I don't know" is the best answer. But if you can say "I believe" it gives children a promise in a future that can be looked forward to and in a Creator or Greater Power they can trust. Death is a "loss of innocence" and we have to find that trust again.

For me now, I see this is the time to live our faith. The fact is that we will all experience the change in our bodies which we call death. But I believe God has a plan for all creatures, as Monsignor Tosti stated, "more wonderful than we could ever imagine."

"If there ever comes a day when we can't be together, keep me in your heart, I'll stay there forever."

—Winnie the Pooh

Rebecca — August 1992

11
Hope

JULY 1994

In July, I decided to have a ceremony at the gravesite for Oliver. Because he had missed the wake and funerals, I wanted to do something. I invited family and some close friends. Father Tosti and my brother John both spoke. Oliver seemed to be listening, but I couldn't tell if he really understood or was absorbing anything. Friends sang a special song they had written called *Angel Friend*. I played a tape of *Hero* and *Dancing with the Lord* for Rebecca, and Doug's friend Peter played *Into the Mystic* for Doug.

Even the bright summer sun could not keep our tears from falling. We were still in disbelief that Doug, Robin, and Rebecca were not here among us.

AUGUST 18, 1994

On Rebecca's twelfth birthday I was once again at the cemetery. I brought with me a blank journal called "Reflections" and started writing:

Dear Rebecca,

Happy 12th Birthday! I never thought I'd be sitting at your grave on this day. Your birthdays were always so special to you and to me. I always wanted them to be perfect. I miss you so much, my precious angel. Giving birth to you was one of the best experiences of my life. You gave me the gift of love. I am forever grateful for that. I promise you, I will continue to shine your light on earth as I receive your light and love every moment. I love you. I miss you. I am proud of you. I know you are taking care of all those babies who have died suddenly like you. I know, somehow your soul knew you were leaving. I can't wait to see you again. Your physical body was as beautiful as your soul. I miss your smile, your cuddles, cutting the crust off your bread, finding your yellow ribbons, waking up to your voice every morning. I know I've been busy with Oliver and I know you understand. Please forgive me if I wasn't always there for you. I'm sorry I was so fearful. I'm trying to not be like that. Please help me. It's so hard to understand all of this. I know Daddy feels really bad. Please tell him I love him. I always have. He is and was a wonderful father. You were such sunshine to us.

Please forgive him too. He wanted the best for you and
Oliver.

Your friends all miss you. I'm going to dinner
tonight with Meghan, Jackie, Stacy and Oliver. We will
celebrate you! I love you, Mom

Oliver's hair had been getting long, and one hot, humid
day in August, he decided he wanted to get his hair cut. My
friend Mary found a barber in Falmouth who was willing to
come to the house. As Oliver stood in his green body cast
holding onto the kitchen sink, Dick gave him, at his request,
an almost shaved head. Once again, I was touched by the
kindness. This man took time out of his busy schedule to help
a boy who needed him. The haircut made him look older and
more serious. It felt like a new Oliver was emerging. Where
was my sweet little boy with the silky, curly brown hair? His
childhood changed forever, Oliver was moving forward and
showing me the way.

September came much too quickly. It was time for all three
of us to re-enter life. Stacy left for Martha's Vineyard to do
her student teaching for her senior year at Wheelock. Oliver
went back to school and started the fourth grade. It was so
hard to shop for school clothes. I kept seeing things Rebecca
would like. She would have been in the seventh grade at the
brand new middle school she had watched being built. She
was so excited to be in the first class to attend. I watched
the bus go by the house without her. It was one of my worst
moments. Rebecca loved school—her friends, her teachers,

the activities, and the challenge of learning. It didn't seem possible she was gone. I would never buy her new school clothes again. She would never ride the bus again.

I started back two days a week at my job as a nutritionist for the Cape Cod WIC Program. I had loved working with the infants and children, taking heights and weights and talking with their mothers about good food habits. But now everything reminded me of Rebecca. I also wanted to be home for Oliver after school. He had been in the after-school program since first grade. It made for a long day. I took an extended leave of absence. We needed each other.

My life revolved around Oliver. We had a quiet, sad Christmas, and then Stacy and I took him to Disneyworld the day after to help cheer us all up. The trip was a gift from our community after a special fundraiser for Oliver. It was a good distraction, but our hearts weren't really in it.

*   *   *

JUNE 2020

I believe in God's plan. I don't always understand it. I've stopped trying. I have asked God so many times "Why?" – I would scream, "It isn't fair. It doesn't make sense. I'm a good person. Rebecca and Oliver were everything to me. Why?"

Shortly after the accident, when we started seeing people again, my friend Brenda gave me a poem in a little wood frame.

Be patient toward all that is
Unsolved in your heart
And try to love the questions themselves.
Do not now seek the answers that cannot
be given you.
Because you would not be able to live them.
And the point is to live everything now.
Perhaps you will gradually,
Without noticing it,
Live along some distant day
Into the answer.

—Rainer Maria Rilke

At first, I rejected this poem and was not comforted. I didn't want to be patient. I wanted to know why. But I kept it and every now and then would read it. Now I see the wisdom in it. I still do not have all the answers. But I am learning to "live everything now." And I am seeing the Divine blueprint more clearly.

"Now is the most important time
because it is the only time
we have any power."

—Leo Tolstoy

12
Guilt

That spring, we went to visit Doug's family in New Mexico and Arizona. They wanted to see Oliver and I thought it would help him to see his grandparents, aunts, uncles, and cousins. They were his connection to Doug. Oliver's best friend, Nathaniel, and his mother, Kathy, went with us to make it more fun and to help us with all the travel. We did have lots of adventures. We went to the Rio Grande Zoo in Albuquerque, traveled through many vast deserts and Indian reservations, and spent time in Sedona and Phoenix. We saw the Grand Canyon during an unexpected snowstorm. Standing at the edge, I thought how vast our world is and how small we are in comparison.

On the flight home to Boston, I was sitting next to Oliver. A young woman sat on my other side. We started talking. She was from Canada and was on her way home from business in Texas. She asked if Oliver was my son. I said yes, and I asked if she had children. She said she had three daughters and was anxious to get home to them. I felt the need to tell her about

Rebecca. Even now, I don't share my story often because I find it bothers people. But once in a while, especially if someone asks how many children I have, it feels as if I have no choice. It is always right there at the surface. Sometimes it's all I can do not to scream, "Don't you know what happened to me and to my family?" This woman was open and easy to talk to, and for some reason, I felt she needed to hear my story. She said it was strange, she had heard the song *Only the Good Die Young* on the radio on the way to the airport. It touched her for some reason and stayed with her, but it also had increased her need to be home with her children. I talked a lot about Rebecca and what a great kid she was. It felt good to share with someone who cared. After we finished talking, I noticed Oliver had been listening, too.

It was a couple of days later when I realized the impact that conversation had had on Oliver. He was playing outside. A group of neighborhood boys had come over. I still watched him constantly out the window. The boys seemed so rough and reckless to me. At one point, afraid he might get hurt, I called him in. I told him sharply to calm down and not be so wild. All of sudden he started crying. He yelled at me.

"Do you wish Rebecca had lived and I died?"

I gasped. "Oh honey, how could you say that?"

"Because she was so good," he cried.

I started crying too. I pulled him to me and held him tight.

"Oliver, I love you both so much, I could never choose between you. Sure, sometimes when you are wild and noisy and climbing trees too high, I think of little girls jumping rope or playing dolls. But that doesn't mean I would choose Rebecca over you or you over Rebecca. It's like if I asked you would you rather have Dad be alive instead of me? I'm sure there are times you get upset with me.

I'm not Daddy. I can't do a lot of the things Dad did with you. Just like you can't be Rebecca for me. I love you and will always love you and take care of you. I don't know why you lived and they died. But we have to be strong and go on without them, together. Don't ever feel bad about missing Rebecca and Dad or about living. Just be you. You were saved for a reason. I needed you. We will always have each other."

Many years ago, I had seen the movie *Sophie's Choice*. I had always been haunted by it. When I watched it, Oliver had been three and Rebecca was five, the same age and gender as Sophie's children were when the Nazi soldiers forced her to choose one to live and one to send to the gas chamber. I was horrified. How could a mother choose between her two children? I knew it would destroy her, and it did. I had no choice about which child I lost. Thank God. But I don't understand why.

I hoped what I said to Oliver helped him. I had read a little on survivor's guilt, and I know it was difficult for him in those first few years. There were nights he missed them so much he cried himself to sleep saying he wished he had died too. And my heart would break again.

*   *   *

JUNE 2020

Everyone's path of healing is different. The hard part is accepting and walking through the pain. Although it is an inner journey mostly done alone, there is help if you are ready and open to it. It takes time and love and support. Oliver and I continue to heal in our own ways to this day. After the accident, I took him to "Kids Grieve Too," a local support group for grieving children, and then to many therapists and healers. I tried to take his pain away by giving him material things that seemed to help for the moment. I took him on trips, snowboarding and hiking. I drove him to karate and drum lessons. And I loved him. His path has been a Herculean effort full of obstacles and difficulties. His strength and courage continue to amaze me. I so admire the man and father he is today.

"Come to the edge," he said.

They said, "We are afraid."

"Come to the edge," he said.

They came.

He pushed them.

And they flew.

—GUILLAUME APOLLINAIRE

Doug and Oliver — November 1992

13
Healing

The first year after the accident, I kept Rebecca and Doug's death at arm's length. I wouldn't, couldn't, go there. I was afraid of the pain and did everything I could to avoid it. I kept busy. I started slowly working again at my massage practice. I worked on my house. I cleaned out closets, threw things away, and organized. This was especially important after seeing what Doug's parents and mine went through cleaning out his house. One day Doug's house had been full of energy, and then suddenly life stopped and all was still. Someone had to clean, sort, and throw things away, all while in a great deal of pain. I wanted to live more simply so someone would not have to do that for me. I decided to brighten up my home and painted the inside walls with soft, warm colors and the outside with bright and cheerful colors. I wanted to create a safe, warm, and happy place for Oliver and me. I could do that with my home, but I wasn't ready to work on my broken heart.

I tried a few therapists. One of those therapists told me it would be three to five years before my life would feel livable again. I was shocked. Three to five years seemed like such a long time to get beyond this. I knew nothing about grief. I had a friend who had lost a child, a cousin whose husband had died, and a young friend whose mother had died. I thought I understood and was compassionate. I had no idea. It felt like a prison sentence. I wonder sometimes if three to five years became a self-fulfilling prophecy for me. It seemed helpful and realistic at the time. I know now that grief is so complex and different for everyone. There are layers. Like nutrition, it is similar but unique for each individual, depending on your background, your beliefs, your body-type, and your personality. I would never tell someone "I know what you are feeling." I don't. I can have compassion, understanding, and love. I can share my experiences so someone does not feel so alone. I can give them hope.

I had also seen an art therapist and a bioenergetics therapist. They both seemed to be as overwhelmed as I was with the enormity of my loss. One just cried the whole session. They didn't seem to help. Although I enjoyed the painting, I was still feeling numb. Maybe it was too soon. And joy still seemed illusive. I focused on Oliver. He became my life, my reason for getting up in the morning. I wanted to keep his life familiar and steady and not have him experience any more change.

By a series of coincidences, I finally connected with the therapist who would become my guide on the road to healing. During the summer of 1995, my friend Brenda fixed me up on a blind date with Richard, a therapist from Salem, Massachusetts, who had been visiting her on Cape Cod. It was much too soon in my grief process to be dating. I babbled on about the accident and Rebecca. But during brunch he told me about a wonderful grief therapist in Newton. Her name was Paula D'Arcy. She was the author of one of the books that Jane had given me, *Song for Sarah*. Paula's daughter, Sarah, and her husband, Roy, were killed by a drunk driver. Paula and her unborn baby were the only survivors of the accident.

Richard and I realized that we had been destined to meet so I could connect with Paula. A couple of days later, I called her and started seeing her soon after that. Normally, she would not see someone who lived so far away—it was an hour-and-a-half drive—but my experience was so similar to hers, it felt right. I was relieved to finally find someone who understood the horror of my sudden loss, but who had not allowed her tragedy to destroy her. I was determined to do the same. I wanted Oliver and me to get the most out of life, to enjoy it, and to live, for ourselves and for Doug, Robin, and Rebecca. It was a strange coincidence too, that Paula's accident happened on August 18, 1975, seven years before Rebecca was born on August 18, 1982.

We shared so much. I could only hope to grow as Paula did. She became my mentor. She helped me see and work on other issues that I had to examine to get to the grief. One of these was a lifelong pattern of avoiding my feelings. I kept busy, being a human "doing" instead of a human "being." I also allowed other people and their opinions to control my life. I had lost myself and my voice.

Over school vacation in February 1996, Oliver and I went skiing and snowboarding in Stowe, Vermont, with our friends Kathy, Nate, and his older sister, Melissa. Driving home, I decided to turn the car around so the kids could see a snow sculpture someone had made in their yard. The man in the car behind us didn't see my blinker because the sun was in his eyes. His car hit us hard in the back near where Oliver sat on the driver's side, in the same place he had been in Doug's car. He hit his head and started screaming. He was having flashbacks. The sound of the crash, together with his screams, frightened us all. No one was really hurt, just very shaken up. All I could do was hold Oliver and try to calm him down. An hour or so later after all the accident reports had been filled out, we were allowed to leave. My car had been dented and the muffler was hanging off, but I could drive. Oliver would not get back in the car. It took a lot of persuading. Kathy and I finally were able to cushion him between Nate and Melissa. By now it was late and we had a five-hour trip home. It was a long night. After an hour, I could no longer drive; reality was hitting me. Kathy took over. Although it was getting late, Oliver refused to sleep or even close his eyes. We finally made it home. It was two days before Oliver and I could leave the security and safety of our home. I wondered if we would ever feel safe in the world again.

My mom continued to drive me to see Paula D'Arcy in Newton twice a month. I don't think I could have done it without her company and support. We would always stop and have lunch at Whole Foods. It was good to have her with me. I continued working on myself, delving into the past, my marriage, my patterns and beliefs. But I still kept that deep pain and sadness buried within. I did not want to go there. Eventually my body decided for me. Paula would later describe it as analogous to holding a beach ball under the water. When the pressure is too much it pops up to the surface. I was holding so much in: the pain of losing Doug and Rebecca, the trauma of Oliver's physical and mental injuries, the responsibility of becoming a single parent, my loss of innocence (tragedy happens to other people), the loss of a job I loved (it was too painful to work with children). All my relationships were changing as well. It was overwhelming.

On April 1, 1996, I woke up in the middle of the night to a popping sensation in my head. Then the room started spinning like a top. I was terrified. I immediately became nauseous and crawled to the bathroom. Finally, the sensation began to subside and I made it back to bed. Although that initial experience was the worst, the vertigo continued for two years, changing form. It's hard to describe. When I had a spell, I felt as if I were on a boat in the fog, unsteady and unsure. Nights were the worst. The bed would feel like it was churning beneath me. I could only lie on my stomach and hold on. If I didn't move, eventually the swaying in my head would subside, and I could sleep only to be awakened in a little while to the same experience. That made for a long night. My anxiety would build, and that increased the sensation. I just wanted to curl up on my side and sleep normally again. Sleeping had been my escape. In the beginning, I would sleep a lot and deeply, like the dead. Now even that was taken away.

As the second anniversary approached, I also developed chronic sinus infections. The congestion in my sinus seemed to relate to the thousands of tears I had not been able to shed. I also had terrible fatigue. I would hit a wall at around 5:00 or 6:00 p.m. Everything would be a major effort after that. Many phone calls went unanswered or unreturned. I knew I had to face the pain. My body demanded it. But how?

I started building puzzles, beautiful ones, 1,000 pieces or more. As a child, I had loved puzzles. They were fun and challenging. Puzzle building became a sort of therapy as well as a diversion. It occupied my mind and kept me focused, but it wasn't terribly taxing. Stacy would join me at this, and we spent many evenings talking and listening to music as we worked. Butterflies, landscapes, angels—they were all so big and beautiful. We would glue and frame many of them. One of my friends felt that puzzle building was a metaphor for my life. I was trying to put the pieces back together. Maybe she was right.

I struggled through the summer of 1996. The vertigo made going to the beach almost impossible. For some reason the sun and heat made it worse. The waves and water mimicked my condition. I could only sit for short periods under an umbrella. Paula was trying to help me slow down and spend time alone with my pain and my thoughts. My friend Anne offered me a few days at her lovely cottage on the beach in Wells, Maine. It would give me a chance to just "be." I rested, walked, prayed, and did some writing, but mostly I felt sad. I would see little girls with long blond hair and watch them wistfully. A lot of my energy was spent fighting my fears and grief. It was still easier to push the pain aside.

I continued on. I worked at my massage practice when I could. I had a brief but disappointing relationship with a man who had been a teacher at the massage school I had attended. He could not handle the emotional pain I carried of losing a child. If you can't process your feelings, how are you going to process the worst feeling of all? Grief clung to me, like an unwanted shroud. Unfortunately, it was two years before he could explain this to me. It was another loss for me.

*   *   *

JUNE 2020

I've learned that life is a process, a journey. Often, we are in a rush to get to our destination and accomplish our goals. Before the accident, I used to say to my friends, "I want to see the five-year plan." Not anymore. I understand now the importance of timing. There is Divine Timing. We often don't know when things will happen. I see that now as a gift. It helps me to live in the present and enjoy life. It is the small moments of joy and laughter and love that make the journey of life so wonderful and powerful.

Time does heal. I had been familiar with Elisabeth Kubler-Ross's work with grief for years before the accident. She describes the five stages of grief as Denial, Anger, Bargaining, Depression, and Acceptance. These stages can happen in any order. You may only experience one or two of them, or none. I can look back and see how long I stayed in denial and bargaining. Bargaining is negotiating to avoid the grief and all the "what if's." I still have work to do with anger. Anger always frightened me. I taught myself not to get angry and push away uncomfortable feelings. At first, after the accident, I was in shock and did not feel anger. It took everything I had to get through the days. Then it became easier to get mad at Doug, and that didn't help. I've read that anger can be a strength to connect you to reality, like a bridge. Maybe. But I'd rather feel love than anger. I'm doing better with acceptance. It's not okay that Rebecca and Doug died, but I'm going to be okay. There were always good and bad days, but now there are mostly good days.

"Pooh, How do you spell love?"
"You don't spell love, Piglet, you feel it."
—WINNIE THE POOH

14
Forgiveness

SEPTEMBER 1996

At the end of the summer, I knew it was time to start going through Rebecca's room to take it apart for Oliver. Rebecca's room was bigger and had a skylight. Oliver was cramped in a tiny bedroom while her empty room remained a shrine, a constant reminder that she was never coming home to it. Paula agreed the move would help me to heal and to face reality. And, as Paula explained, it would give Oliver the message that he was important. It would help him to let go of the past, too. It became a six-month ordeal.

First, I took photos of her room to keep my memories from fading. Paula suggested I get a chest for Rebecca's special things. I found one immediately in a catalog. It was Southwestern, of course, with bright colored stripes and designs. It was perfect. I put in Kermit, the crocheted frog she had had since she was a baby, and her mint-green ballet costume for the recital she never got to dance at. I was sure she had tried it on and twirled around in it. I gathered her poetry, songs, and letters, her favorite shirt, pictures, the dress she wore to her father's wedding, her worn and faded jeans, and her lobster earrings, and carefully placed them in the chest. I got boxes and folded her clothes. Some I gave away, most I couldn't bear to part with yet. I thought maybe someday I would make a quilt from her best-loved shirts, pants, dresses, and costumes. I sorted through her books, keeping most of them. Each item had a memory, a reminder of a part of her life. I carefully folded the teal and purple curtains I had sewed for her because she wanted ones just like mine. Rebecca had five American Girl dolls that her Aunt Tara had given her each Christmas since she was seven. She loved those dolls. A couple had haircuts and polish on their nails and all were well worn from so much attention. I didn't think I could ever part with them. She also had a troll collection, some from my own childhood. She had wonderful tapes of herself reading books, singing songs, pretending to be a radio announcer. I treasure those tapes of her voice. All her games—Uno, Perfect Match, Scrabble, and Life—were set aside for Oliver.

One day I was cleaning and going through Rebecca's things, listening to her voice on tape and feeling very sad. I had already been in her closet a couple times that morning and many times in the past months. As I opened it again, a little note fluttered down to my feet. I picked it up. She often left little love notes for me or her Dad. She had drawn a small rainbow and had written:

I love you mom, Terece Twitchell Horton.

Love Rebecca

"Thank you, Rebecca," I whispered. Then I fell to the floor and sobbed.

In January 1997, I painted her pink walls blue and we finally moved Oliver in. He loved her waterbed and adjusted quickly to his new room. It felt right.

I continued my healing by having massages, Reiki, acupuncture, homeopathy, and therapy sessions with Paula. I strived to keep my stress level down. The fatigue continued, but the vertigo was better. When I felt up to it, I worked at my massage practice. My faithful clients were supportive and understanding. I felt that things were going well.

One day in April 1997, I finally called Jim Kelley. Jim was the police officer who had given me his card at the trial of the drunk driver who had killed Doug, Robin, and Rebecca. He told me to call him someday when I was up to it. He was the first on the scene of the accident and wanted to tell me what happened. I took his card and put it in my checkbook. I looked at it every time I wrote a check, knowing I needed to call him. He was glad to hear from me. We made arrangements for him to come to my house to talk to me and see Oliver again.

I listened carefully to Jim's story. It almost seemed that he was talking about strangers—not my daughter, not my family. At one point as he got emotional, I comforted him. I was quite upset too, but as usual I pushed the pain inside and acted as if I was fine. It meant so much that he cared and was there for Rebecca when she died and also helped Oliver to hold on. Thank you, Jim.

A couple of days later, I was at work and giving a massage to an elderly client. All of a sudden, I felt hot and a little nauseous. I passed out cold and, dropped to the floor. The client had to jump off the table, throw on some clothes, and run upstairs to another office to call an ambulance. I woke up a few minutes later to the kind face of an EMT. I was confused and thought I was in my bed waking up in the morning. My bladder had let go and I couldn't understand why I was wet. After a thorough exam and a CAT Scan at Cape Cod Hospital, they told me they could not find any physical reason for my collapse. I was released after a few hours of observation.

I knew my body was speaking to me. I had to feel my emotions to start releasing some of the sadness and pain. As a massage therapist, I was aware of the body-mind connection. Mental and emotional tension can manifest itself physically, and over a period of time it blocks energy and affects our health and well-being. I had often referred to Louise Hay's book *You Can Heal Your Body*. In it she lists the correlation between a symptom or dis-ease and its likely emotional cause. I looked up *fainting*. I learned that it was probably caused by fear and the inability to cope. The new thought pattern or affirmation she suggested told me that I have the inner strength to handle everything in my life.

I knew I needed time and stillness. I decided to take the summer of 1997 off completely and give myself space for healing. I also felt I needed more time to be with Oliver.

*   *   *

JUNE 20, 2020

After that summer, I went back to work as a massage therapist and eventually worked part time at WIC again for another ten years. I never fainted or experienced the vertigo or sinus infections again. I began passionately learning more about the body and how our emotions affect our health and happiness.

In her book *Your Body Speaks your Mind*, Deb Shapiro writes about making a choice to heal and work with the vulnerable parts of ourselves. Our bodies strive to stay in balance, in homeostasis. An illness or injury can be the way the body is trying to handle an imbalance. After reading her book, I could see more clearly the walls I had built around myself. By staying busy, putting other people's needs first, repressing my feelings, and not expressing my own needs, I protected myself with my self-imposed armor. But by keeping out the pain and fear, the armor was also a barrier to joy and love.

I looked at my belief systems and deep-seated patterns of thinking and behavior. I started questioning and changing some of my beliefs and honoring my feelings. I began to slowly surrender and trust life again. I prayed and meditated more. To this day, I continue to work at opening my heart.

In 2006, I started training in Craniosacral Therapy, a light touch approach that works with the central nervous system to release tensions. This allows the entire body to relax and self-correct. As a craniosacral therapist, I treat my clients' physical symptoms and also relieve the stresses that are hidden in their bodies. I believe our bodies have the answers. We have to be still and listen.

Healing involves discovering our inner strength—this was the message in the song Rebecca sang to me before she died. But it takes time and dedication.

Another very important part of healing is forgiveness. There are many definitions of forgiveness, but I like *to make peace with.* We forgive to heal ourselves. It doesn't mean we must forget the behavior, but we can forgive the person who hurt us. We are human and we all make mistakes. When we forgive someone, we take back our power. This gives us more energy and makes more room for love in our hearts.

As I write this, I am thinking of the drunk driver who killed three members of my family. I know on some level I forgive him, but I've never told him that. I know he didn't get up that morning and plan to murder three people and destroy the lives of all who loved them. He has to wake up every morning and live with that, a prison sentence in itself. He was incarcerated for twelve years.

In the beginning days after the accident, I never had any energy to think of him. At first, my family kept hidden from me all newspapers with the sensational headlines about the accident and the three-day manhunt. I could only be with Oliver and try to deal with losing my family. I had no room for anger in my heart or body. Even breathing was a struggle at times.

The trial was in March of 1995. I did attend, but it was more like an out-of-body experience. I read my victim impact statement. This allows crime victims the opportunity to speak during the sentencing of the convicted person. I tried to capture their lives in a few words, who they were and what they meant to me. This wasn't enough. It didn't ease any of the pain of losing Rebecca, Doug, and Robin and seeing Oliver suffer. When I began writing this book, I sent the "drunk driver" a letter:

February 3, 1999

Dear _____,

I have not thought much about you these past three years. I have been busy rebuilding my life and my son's life which were shattered by the death of my daughter, my ex-husband and his wife.

I know you have a family, too. I know you have had a lot of time to think. I wonder how you have dealt with this. I understand you will be a free man in 2005 and will have another chance at life. Something Doug, Robin and Rebecca will never have. How will you live the new life you are being given?"

You may respond to me,   Terece Horton

I wasn't sure what kind of response I was looking for but I know I needed some kind of an apology. The choices he made that day ruined so many lives and families. A few months later I received this reply as printed here:

November 1999

"Dear Terece Horton,

I have thought a lot about you and your son, each and every day during these passed years. I also have been busy trying to rebuild my families life.

I know there is not anything that I can say, that will make your pain any less, I would like you to know that, I am truly sorry. I understand the depth of my misdeed, I wish there was something I could do to make your world a little better.

I to have a family and I would not know what to do if someone took my family from me, and that's what makes this situation hard for me to deal with, see I wish that it was me instead of your family.

I've taken all possible steps to never repeat this kind of behavior that lead to this. See I've been taking A/A and N/A substance abuse classes in here, I'm also involved in other programs that help me understand who I am, and what made me do the things I did.

I intend to do the best that I am capable of, and I will never do anything to compromise my stability. I truly am remorseful towards that incident, because I know what it is to have people that you care dearly about and have them taken away, by some idiot like me.

I know in my heart the tragedy that I have been! God willing I will never be that person that I was, I can guarantee that I will never do anything to endanger anyone's family let alone break a family apart, because I know the importance of family.

I think about that incident every single day, and it pains me to know what I've done, not just to you, but to everyone we love. I hope that in the future I can help others, by speaking about topics that can lead them down the wrong road.

I would like to speak to the young children, in are schools and also at organized meetings so I can share my experiences and the pain that comes with making the wrong choices.

I appreciate you writing, you gave me a chance to respond thank you very much.

Sincerely, _____"

I'm not sure I accepted his apology in my heart at that time. Although satisfied to get a response, I didn't feel much relief, and his words didn't seem to soften my sadness. I was still pretty numb. Now, twenty-three years later, reading that letter again, I see and feel differently. I can accept his apology and feel his pain. I hope he has kept his word to live a better life. I do not know and do not feel a need to know.

> **"Forgiveness is a reflection of loving yourself**
> **enough to move on."**
> —DR. STEVE MARABOLI

15
Love

One thing we know:
Our God is the same
This earth is precious to Him....
All things are connected.

—CHIEF SEATTLE

We are all part of something greater than ourselves. Our actions affect so many people, yet we are often unaware of our place in the link. Not only are we connected, but also we need each other. This accident changed so many lives. It was almost as if people were placed in certain positions—to play their roles. Suzanne supported me all the way home when I could barely stand. Tara and Jane went to Oliver to be with him until I could get there. Jim Kelley arrived at the crash and was there for Rebecca and Oliver. The rescue personnel carefully cut Oliver out of the metal. Sister Claire sat at Oliver's hospital bed, praying until someone came.

We never know the impact the choices and decisions we make can have on someone else. I can, once again, see the Divine Plan and the Divine Timing here. Robin was not supposed to go to New Hampshire. She was going to stay home, rest, plant flowers, and have some time for herself. What changed her mind? Jeff Chase did a favor for another police officer and took her four to eight a.m. shift. He was instrumental in finding me quickly because he knew me. Meghan, Rebecca's best friend, was supposed to go to New Hampshire with them but a missed phone call kept her home . . . and safe. Doug never left the Cape on Memorial Day weekend. He would say, "There's no need. We have everything here." He always had a cookout to celebrate the arrival of summer. Why did he make an exception this time?

I know I can never answer these questions. But I can focus on the loving generosity of my family and friends who stopped their daily life to be with us. It still brings tears to my eyes. I can see how many lives Rebecca's life touched and changed. I can see that kindness has a ripple effect. Two years after the accident, I wrote thank you notes to my family, friends, and all I knew who gave us their time and love. There were so many unseen helpers . . . but maybe this is a chance to express my heartfelt gratitude to the ones I didn't know. To everyone who sent money, planted flowers, brought food, prayed, and gave their time, skills, and help: Thank you! You are all truly earth angels! And thank you to all my heavenly angels! I know you were with me too.

It took me a long time to see Rebecca's gifts. Paula D'Arcy once said to me during a session, "You believe in

God, but you trust Terece." At first, I was puzzled, but over the years the words often popped into my head. And now I understand. When I trust God, miracles happen. I let go of "my way."

The messages and gifts keep coming. I don't doubt them. It feels as if she is saying hello. One of my favorites is 8-18, her birthday. I'll look up and see those numbers on a license plate or glance at the clock and it's 8:18. When I fall back into sadness, I find something to be grateful for, and I stay in the present moment. When I trust in the higher power that is always at work in my life, my faith grows and my awareness of the blessing of God deepens.

Knowing I was approaching the end of this book, I started looking in my special chest for some photos to add, and I found this very worn, folded-up note from Rebecca. She knew I was always working on self-improvement and had given me this note a few months before she died. On the outside of the paper she had written:

> To Mom, Love Rebecca
> I know you will like this.
> Open this by yourself somewhere

I carefully opened the note, remembering that I had carried it in my wallet for many years. It was her list of affirmations for me:

I can do anything

I am strong

There is nothing I can fear

Everybody loves me

I am the most loving person in the world

I can never get hurt because I am strong

There is nothing to worry about

Everything is alright

Nothing is perfect

I am great

I am fearless

I am powerful

Yes!

It was another reminder that she is always with me, another reminder of how well she knew me and my fears. Affirmations help you stay positive and focus your thoughts on what you want instead of what you fear. You can choose what you think about and how you feel. It is not always easy and takes practice, but is magical when you get it right.

The 2020 pandemic and the order to "shelter in place" gave me the time to stop the busyness and pause and to reflect on my life and what really matters. I feel I was guided by Rebecca to finish this book that I started over twenty-three years ago. I had worked on it for at least three years but hadn't been sure how to end it. Then life got in the way and I put it in a box. Now it felt right to finish it.

By sharing Rebecca's story and all the lives she touched, I am reminded again that Love never dies. Writing and remembering all the wonderful memories has helped me let go of big bags of sadness that I didn't even know I was still carrying around. She has shown me in so many ways to choose joy and to always look for the mirabilia and messages! They are there. Thank you, my sweet daughter, for your gift of Love.

Telling our story has also helped me find my voice. I feel this quote describes my life.

And the day came when the risk to remain tight in a bud became more painful than the risk it took to blossom.

—ANAÏS NIN

My heart, like a red rose, opens more every day. Sometimes when I'm walking along, I can almost feel Rebecca slip her hand in mine, as she did so many times. And I smile and feel her joy. And every so often, I can see Rebecca's light shining through my grandson's eyes.

Perfect Love Casts Out Fear

Love, Love, Love . . . Always Love